DOVER · THRI

King John

William Shakespeare

DOVER PUBLICATIONS, INC.
Mineola, New York

DOVER THRIFT EDITIONS

GENERAL EDITOR: MARY CAROLYN WALDREP
EDITOR OF THIS VOLUME: ALISON DAURIO

Copyright

Theatrical Rights

This Dover Thrift Edition may be used in its entirety, in adaptation, or in any other way for theatrical productions, professional and amateur, in the United States, without fee, permission, or acknowledgment. (This may not apply outside of the United States, as copyright conditions may vary.)

Bibliographical Note

This Dover edition, first published in 2015, contains the unabridged text of *King John,* as published in Volume XI of *The Caxton Edition of the Complete Works of William Shakespeare,* Caxton Publishing Company, London, n.d. The introductory Note was prepared specially for this edition, and the explanatory footnotes from the Caxton edition have been revised.

International Standard Book Number

ISBN-13: 978-0-486-79693-2
ISBN-10: 0-486-79693-0

Manufactured in the United States by Courier Corporation
79693001   2015
www.doverpublications.com

Note

WILLIAM SHAKESPEARE (1564–1616) was born in Stratford-on-Avon, Warwickshire, England. Although much of his early life remains sketchy, it is known that he moved to London around 1589 to earn his way as an actor and playwright. He joined an acting company known as Lord Chamberlain's Men in 1594, a decision that finally enabled him to share in the financial success of his plays. Only eighteen of his thirty-seven plays were published during his lifetime and these were usually sold directly to theater companies and printed in quartos, or single-play editions, without his approval.

Written around 1594–96, this work chronicles the rule of the often criticized King John of England. The play commences as King John learns of the betrayal of his nephew Arthur, who has aligned with the French king in order to usurp the throne. This is only the beginning of his difficulties. Full of treachery and dramatic battle scenes, the play explores the events leading up to the eventual demise of the ill-fated king.

DRAMATIS PERSONÆ

KING JOHN.

PRINCE HENRY, son to the king.

ARTHUR, Duke of Bretagne, nephew to the king.

The Earl of PEMBROKE.

The Earl of ESSEX.

The Earl of SALISBURY.

The LORD BIGOT.

HUBERT DE BURGH.

ROBERT FAULCONBRIDGE, son to Sir Robert Faulconbridge.

PHILIP the BASTARD, his half-brother.

JAMES GURNEY, servant to Lady Faulconbridge.

PETER of Pomfret, a prophet.

PHILIP, King of France.

LEWIS, the Dauphin.

LYMOGES, Duke of Austria.

CARDINAL PANDULPH, the Pope's legate.

MELUN, a French lord.

CHATILLON, ambassador from France to King John.

QUEEN ELINOR, mother to King John.

CONSTANCE, mother to Arthur.

BLANCH of Spain, niece to King John.

LADY FAULCONBRIDGE.

Lords, Citizens of Angiers, Sheriff, Heralds, Officers, Soldiers, Messengers, and other Attendants.

SCENE: *Partly in England, and partly in France*

ACT I.
Scene I. *King John's Palace.*

Enter King John, Queen Elinor, Pembroke, Essex,
Salisbury, *and others, with* Chatillon

King John. Now, say, Chatillon, what would France with us?
  Chat. Thus, after greeting, speaks the King of France
In my behaviour to the majesty,
The borrowed majesty, of England here.
  Eli. A strange beginning: "borrowed majesty!"
  K. John. Silence, good mother; hear the embassy.
  Chat. Philip of France, in right and true behalf
Of thy deceased brother Geffrey's son,
Arthur Plantagenet, lays most lawful claim
To this fair island and the territories,   10
To Ireland, Poictiers, Anjou, Touraine, Maine,
Desiring thee to lay aside the sword
Which sways usurpingly these several titles,
And put the same into young Arthur's hand,
Thy nephew and right royal sovereign.
  K. John. What follows if we disallow of this?
  Chat. The proud control of fierce and bloody war,
To enforce these rights so forcibly withheld.
  K. John. Here have we war for war and blood for
         blood,
Controlment for controlment: so answer France.   20
  Chat. Then take my king's defiance from my mouth,
The farthest limit of my embassy.

---

3 *In my behaviour*] In my person.
17 *control*] coercion, compulsion.

1

K. JOHN. Bear mine to him, and so depart in peace:
Be thou as lightning in the eyes of France;
For ere thou canst report I will be there,
The thunder of my cannon shall be heard:
So hence! Be thou the trumpet of our wrath
And sullen presage of your own decay.
An honourable conduct let him have.
Pembroke, look to 't. Farewell, Chatillon.   30

　　　　　　　　　　[*Exeunt Chatillon and Pembroke.*

　ELI. What now, my son! have I not ever said
How that ambitious Constance would not cease
Till she had kindled France and all the world,
Upon the right and party of her son?
This might have been prevented and made whole
With very easy arguments of love,
Which now the manage of two kingdoms must
With fearful bloody issue arbitrate.
　K. JOHN. Our strong possession and our right for us.
　ELI. Your strong possession much more than your right,   40
Or else it must go wrong with you and me:
So much my conscience whispers in your ear,
Which none but heaven and you and I shall hear.

Enter a Sheriff

　ESSEX. My liege, here is the strangest controversy
Come from the country to be judged by you,
That e'er I heard: shall I produce the men?
　K. JOHN. Let them approach.
Our abbeys and our priories shall pay
This expedition's charge.

Enter ROBERT FAULCONBRIDGE, *and* PHILIP *his bastard brother*

　　　　　　　What men are you?
　BAST. Your faithful subject I, a gentleman   50

---

26 *cannon*] Shakespeare, characteristically indifferent to strict historical accuracy, antedates the use of gunpowder by nearly a century and a half. John's reign began in 1199. Cannon are said to have been first employed at the battle of Crécy in 1346.
28 *sullen presage*] (messenger of) doleful foreboding.
37 *manage*] management, administration, government.

Born in Northamptonshire, and eldest son,
As I suppose, to Robert Faulconbridge,
A soldier, by the honour-giving hand
Of Cœur-de-lion knighted in the field.

K. JOHN. What art thou?

ROB. The son and heir to that same Faulconbridge.

K. JOHN. Is that the elder, and art thou the heir?
You came not of one mother then, it seems.

BAST. Most certain of one mother, mighty king;
That is well known; and, as I think, one father: 60
But for the certain knowledge of that truth
I put you o'er to heaven and to my mother:
Of that I doubt, as all men's children may.

ELI. Out on thee, rude man! thou dost shame thy mother
And wound her honour with this diffidence.

BAST. I, madam? no, I have no reason for it;
That is my brother's plea and none of mine;
The which if he can prove, a' pops me out
At least from fair five hundred pound a year:
Heaven guard my mother's honour and my land!   70

K. JOHN. A good blunt fellow. Why, being younger born,
Doth he lay claim to thine inheritance?

BAST. I know not why, except to get the land.
But once he slander'd me with bastardy:
But whether I be as true begot or no,
That still I lay upon my mother's head;
But that I am as well begot, my liege,—
Fair fall the bones that took the pains for me!—
Compare our faces and be judge yourself.
If old Sir Robert did beget us both   80
And were our father and this son like him,
O old Sir Robert, father, on my knee
I give heaven thanks I was not like to thee!

K. JOHN. Why, what a madcap hath heaven lent us here!

ELI. He hath a trick of Cœur-de-lion's face;
The accent of his tongue affecteth him.

---

62 *put you o'er*] refer you.
65 *diffidence*] distrust.
78 *Fair fall*] Luck befall.
85 *trick*] trace; the word is a heraldic term for a tracing or copy.
86 *affecteth*] smacks of, resembles.

Do you not read some tokens of my son
In the large composition of this man?
   K. JOHN. Mine eye hath well examined his parts
And finds them perfect Richard. Sirrah, speak,   90
What doth move you to claim your brother's land?
   BAST. Because he hath a half-face, like my father.
With half that face would he have all my land:
A half-faced groat five hundred pound a year!
   ROB. My gracious liege, when that my father lived,
Your brother did employ my father much,—
   BAST. Well, sir, by this you cannot get my land:
Your tale must be how he employ'd my mother.
   ROB. And once dispatch'd him in an embassy
To Germany, there with the emperor   100
To treat of high affairs touching that time.
The advantage of his absence took the king
And in the mean time sojourn'd at my father's;
Where how he did prevail I shame to speak,
But truth is truth: large lengths of seas and shores
Between my father and my mother lay,
As I have heard my father speak himself,
When this same lusty gentleman was got.
Upon his death-bed he by will bequeath'd
His lands to me, and took it on his death   110
That this my mother's son was none of his;
And if he were, he came into the world
Full fourteen weeks before the course of time.
Then, good my liege, let me have what is mine,
My father's land, as was my father's will.
   K. JOHN. Sirrah, your brother is legitimate;
Your father's wife did after wedlock bear him,
And if she did play false, the fault was hers;
Which fault lies on the hazards of all husbands
That marry wives. Tell me, how if my brother,   120
Who, as you say, took pains to get this son,
Had of your father claim'd this son for his?

---

94 *groat*] a small silver coin (worth fourpence) stamped with the king's head in
    profile or half-face.
110 *took it on his death*] affirmed it on his deathbed, in the solemn expectation
    of death.
119 *lies … husbands*] is among the risks all husbands run.

In sooth, good friend, your father might have kept
This calf, bred from his cow, from all the world;
In sooth he might; then, if he were my brother's,
My brother might not claim him; nor your father,
Being none of his, refuse him: this concludes;
My mother's son did get your father's heir;
Your father's heir must have your father's land.

ROB. Shall then my father's will be of no force   130
To dispossess that child which is not his?

BAST. Of no more force to dispossess me, sir,
Than was his will to get me, as I think.

ELI. Whether hadst thou rather be a Faulconbridge,
And like thy brother, to enjoy thy land,
Or the reputed son of Cœur-de-lion,
Lord of thy presence and no land beside?

BAST. Madam, an if my brother had my shape,
And I had his, sir Robert's his, like him;
And if my legs were two such riding-rods,   140
My arms such eel-skins stuff'd, my face so thin
That in mine ear I durst not stick a rose
Lest men should say "Look, where three-farthings goes!"
And, to his shape, were heir to all this land,
Would I might never stir from off this place,
I would give it every foot to have this face;
I would not be sir Nob in any case.

ELI. I like thee well: wilt thou forsake thy fortune,
Bequeath thy land to him and follow me?
I am a soldier and now bound to France.   150

BAST. Brother, take you my land, I'll take my chance.
Your face hath got five hundred pound a year,
Yet sell your face for five pence and 't is dear.

---

127 *concludes*] is conclusive.

137 *Lord of thy presence*] Owner of thy fine presence or person.

140 *riding-rods*] thin wands used by horsemen; riding whips.

142 *rose*] Fashionable Elizabethans seem to have occasionally worn roses or
other flowers in their pierced ears. The Bastard refers to this practice rather
than to another and a more common custom of tying rosettes of ribbon
about the ear.

143 *three-farthings*] a very thin silver coin of Queen Elizabeth's day, on the
reverse of which a rose was stamped.

144 *to his shape, were heir*] in addition to his shape, were he heir.

147 *sir Nob*] a nickname for Sir Robert.

153 *your face for five pence*] a penny more than the worth of "a half-faced groat."

Madam, I'll follow you unto the death.

    Eli. Nay, I would have you go before me thither.

    Bast. Our country manners give our betters way.

    K. John. What is thy name?

    Bast. Philip, my liege, so is my name begun;
Philip, good old sir Robert's wife's eldest son.

    K. John. From henceforth bear his name whose form thou
               bear'st: 160
Kneel thou down Philip, but rise more great,
Arise sir Richard and Plantagenet.

    Bast. Brother by the mother's side, give me your hand:
My father gave me honour, yours gave land.
Now blessed be the hour, by night or day,
When I was got, sir Robert was away!

    Eli. The very spirit of Plantagenet!
I am thy grandam, Richard; call me so.

    Bast. Madam, by chance but not by truth; what though?
Something about, a little from the right,   170
    In at the window, or else o'er the hatch:
Who dares not stir by day must walk by night,
    And have is have, however men do catch:
Near or far off, well won is still well shot,
And I am I, howe'er I was begot.

    K. John. Go, Faulconbridge: now hast thou thy desire;
A landless knight makes thee a landed squire.
Come, madam, and come, Richard, we must speed
For France, for France, for it is more than need.

    Bast. Brother, adieu: good fortune come to thee!   180
For thou wast got i' the way of honesty.

                       [Exeunt all but Bastard.

A foot of honour better than I was;
But many a many foot of land the worse.
Well, now can I make any Joan a lady.
"Good den, sir Richard!"—"God-a-mercy, fellow!"—
And if his name be George, I'll call him Peter;

---

170 *Something about … right*] Somewhat deviously, a little off the straight path,
    left-handedly.
171 *In … hatch*] Colloquial euphemisms for illegitimate birth.
177 *A landless knight*] A reference to John's familiar nickname of Lacklands.
185 *Good den*] Good evening.

For new-made honour doth forget men's names;
'T is too respective and too sociable
For your conversion. Now your traveller,
He and his toothpick at my worship's mess, 190
And when my knightly stomach is sufficed,
Why then I suck my teeth and catechize
My picked man of countries: "My dear sir,"
Thus, leaning on mine elbow, I begin,
"I shall beseech you"—that is question now;
And then comes answer like an Absey book:
"O sir," says answer, "at your best command;
At your employment; at your service, sir:"
"No, sir," says question, "I, sweet sir, at yours:"
And so, ere answer knows what question would, 200
Saving in dialogue of compliment,
And talking of the Alps and Apennines,
The Pyrenean and the river Po,
It draws towards supper in conclusion so.
But this is worshipful society,
And fits the mounting spirit like myself;
For he is but a bastard to the time
That doth not smack of observation;
And so am I, whether I smack or no;
And not alone in habit and device, 210
Exterior form, outward accoutrement,
But from the inward motion to deliver
Sweet, sweet, sweet poison for the age's tooth:

188–189 *too respective and too sociable For your conversion*] too considerate (of the feelings of inferiors) and too suggestive of social equality to suit a change from low to high estate.

190 *his toothpick*] obtrusive play with the toothpick was a current affectation of travelled men of fashion.
my worship's mess] my dining table.

193 *picked*] refined, fastidious.

196 *an Absey book*] an A. B. C. book, a primer from which children learnt the alphabet and simple phrases.

201 *dialogue of compliment*] talk consisting of complimentary phrases.

203 *The Pyrenean*] The Pyrenees.

207–208 *For he is ... of observation*] For he is no lawful offspring of the age—he is a mean fellow in the estimate of contemporaries—who does not show signs of having observed or studied foreign customs.

212–213 *from the inward ... age's tooth*] proceeding from, or owing to the inward impulse to please the palate of the age with the extremely sweet poison of flattery.

Which, though I will not practise to deceive,
Yet, to avoid deceit, I mean to learn;
For it shall strew the footsteps of my rising.
But who comes in such haste in riding-robes?
What woman-post is this? hath she no husband
That will take pains to blow a horn before her?

Enter LADY FAULCONBRIDGE *and* JAMES GURNEY

O me! it is my mother. How now, good lady?　　　　220
What brings you here to court so hastily?
　　LADY F. Where is that slave, thy brother? where is he,
That holds in chase mine honour up and down?
　　BAST. My brother Robert? old sir Robert's son?
Colbrand the giant, that same mighty man?
Is it sir Robert's son that you seek so?
　　LADY F. Sir Robert's son! Ay, thou unreverend boy,
Sir Robert's son: why scorn'st thou at sir Robert?
He is sir Robert's son, and so art thou.
　　BAST. James Gurney, wilt thou give us leave awhile?　　230
　　GUR. Good leave, good Philip.
　　BAST.　　　　　　　　Philip! sparrow: James,
There's toys abroad: anon I'll tell thee more.

　　　　　　　　　　　　　　　　　　[*Exit Gurney.*

---

215 *to avoid deceit*] to avoid being misled by other people's deceit, to make
　　myself a match for the cheat.
219 *a horn*] a quibble on the obvious meaning of "post horn" and of the
　　"horns" which a wife's infidelity was commonly said to cause to sprout
　　from a husband's brow.
225 *Colbrand the giant*] A legendary Danish hero, whose overthrow in combat
　　was one of the exploits traditionally assigned to Guy of Warwick.
227 *unreverend*] irreverent.
230 *James Gurney*] Shakespeare may have called this small personage, whom he
　　invented, after Hugues Gournay, a Norman squire, whose land in
　　Normandy King John seized very early in his adventures in France.
　　give us leave] withdraw.
231 *Good leave*] with all good-will.
　　Philip! sparrow] Tut! Don't take me for a sparrow. Philip was the common
　　nickname of the sparrow, the chirp of the bird being thought to resemble
　　the articulation of the word Philip.
232 *toys*] idle tales, worthless rumours.

Madam, I was not old sir Robert's son:
Sir Robert might have eat his part in me
Upon Good-Friday and ne'er broke his fast:
Sir Robert could do well: marry, to confess,
Could he get me? Sir Robert could not do it:
We know his handiwork: therefore, good mother,
To whom am I beholding for these limbs?
Sir Robert never holp to make this leg.   240
    LADY F. Hast thou conspired with thy brother too,
That for thine own gain shouldst defend mine honour?
What means this scorn, thou most untoward knave?
    BAST. Knight, knight, good mother, Basilisco-like.
What! I am dubb'd! I have it on my shoulder.
But, mother, I am not sir Robert's son;
I have disclaim'd sir Robert and my land;
Legitimation, name and all is gone:
Then, good my mother, let me know my father;
Some proper man, I hope: who was it, mother?   250
    LADY F. Hast thou denied thyself a Faulconbridge?
    BAST. As faithfully as I deny the devil.
    LADY F. King Richard Cœur-de-lion was thy father:
By long and vehement suit I was seduced
To make room for him in my husband's bed:
Heaven lay not my transgression to my charge!
Thou art the issue of my dear offence,
Which was so strongly urged past my defence.
    BAST. Now, by this light, were I to get again,
Madam, I would not wish a better father.   260
Some sins do bear their privilege on earth,
And so doth yours; your fault was not your folly:
Needs must you lay your heart at his dispose,

234–235 *eat his part ... his fast*] a proverbial expression implying the negation of action.

236 *to confess*] to come to confession, to make a clean breast of it.

243 *untoward*] unmannerly.

244 *Basilisco-like*] a sarcastic allusion to a braggart named Basilisco in the contemporary play of *Soliman and Perseda*. Basilisco bombastically insists on being addressed as "*knight*" by a farcical servant who mockingly calls him "*knave.*"

257 *dear*] grievous.

261 *Some sins ... earth*] Some sins (despite the punishment allotted them by heaven) are privileged to pass uncensured on earth.

Subjected tribute to commanding love,
Against whose fury and unmatched force
The aweless lion could not wage the fight,
Nor keep his princely heart from Richard's hand.
He that perforce robs lions of their hearts
May easily win a woman's. Ay, my mother,
With all my heart I thank thee for my father!   270
Who lives and dares but say thou didst not well
When I was got, I'll send his soul to hell.
Come, lady, I will show thee to my kin;
    And they shall say, when Richard me begot,
If thou hadst said him nay, it had been sin:
      Who says it was, he lies; I say 't was not.   [*Exeunt.*

266–267 *The aweless ... hand*] A reference to the fable that Richard I owed his
    surname Cœur-de-lion to his having pulled out through the mouth the
    heart of a lion, which was let loose upon him while he was in prison.

ACT II.

Scene I. *France. Before Angiers.*

Enter Austria *and forces, drums, etc. on one side: on the other*
King Philip *of France and his power;* Lewis, Arthur,
Constance *and attendants*

LEWIS. Before Angiers well met, brave Austria.
Arthur, that great forerunner of thy blood,
Richard, that robb'd the lion of his heart
And fought the holy wars in Palestine,
By this brave duke came early to his grave:
And for amends to his posterity,
At our importance hither is he come,
To spread his colours, boy, in thy behalf,
And to rebuke the usurpation
Of thy unnatural uncle, English John: 10
Embrace him, love him, give him welcome hither.

ARTH. God shall forgive you Cœur-de-lion's death
The rather that you give his offspring life,
Shadowing their right under your wings of war:
I give you welcome with a powerless hand,
But with a heart full of unstained love:
Welcome before the gates of Angiers, duke.

LEW. A noble boy! Who would not do thee right?

AUST. Upon thy cheek lay I this zealous kiss,
As seal to this indenture of my love, 20
That to my home I will no more return,
Till Angiers and the right thou hast in France,

---

2 *forerunner*] predecessor.

5 *By this brave duke ... grave*] Shakespeare follows the old play in the error of
making Richard fall by the hand of the Archduke of Austria, to whom the
king owed his famous imprisonment. The archduke predeceased Richard
I. The king was slain four years after his captor's death while besieging the
castle of the Vicomte de Limoges, one of his own vassals. The Archduke
of Austria and the Vicomte de Limoges were two very different beings,
but at III, i, 117. *infra,* "Limoges" and "Austria" are confusedly introduced
as the titles of one and the same person; they figure in like fashion in the
dramatis personæ.

7 *At our importance*] At our importunity, entreaty.

20 *indenture*] binding contract.

11

Together with that pale, that white-faced shore,
Whose foot spurns back the ocean's roaring tides
And coops from other lands her islanders,
Even till that England, hedged in with the main,
That water-walled bulwark, still secure
And confident from foreign purposes,
Even till that utmost corner of the west
Salute thee for her king: till then, fair boy,   30
Will I not think of home, but follow arms.

 CONST. O, take his mother's thanks, a widow's thanks,
Till your strong hand shall help to give him strength
To make a more requital to your love!

 AUST. The peace of heaven is theirs that lift their swords
In such a just and charitable war.

 K. PHI. Well then, to work: our cannon shall be bent
Against the brows of this resisting town.
Call for our chiefest men of discipline,
To cull the plots of best advantages: 40
We'll lay before this town our royal bones,
Wade to the market-place in Frenchmen's blood,
But we will make it subject to this boy.

 CONST. Stay for an answer to your embassy,
Lest unadvised you stain your swords with blood:
My Lord Chatillon may from England bring
That right in peace which here we urge in war,
And then we shall repent each drop of blood
That hot rash haste so indirectly shed.

Enter CHATILLON

 K. PHI. A wonder, lady! lo, upon thy wish,   50
Our messenger Chatillon is arrived!
What England says, say briefly, gentle lord;
We coldly pause for thee; Chatillon, speak.

---

23 *that pale ... shore*] the white cliffs of Albion.
34 *a more*] a greater.
40 *To cull ... advantages*] To select the positions of best advantage for the assault.
45 *unadvised*] in your rashness.
49 *indirectly*] unrighteously.

CHAT. Then turn your forces from this paltry siege
And stir them up against a mightier task.
England, impatient of your just demands,
Hath put himself in arms: the adverse winds,
Whose leisure I have stay'd, have given him time
To land his legions all as soon as I;
His marches are expedient to this town,   60
His forces strong, his soldiers confident.
With him along is come the mother-queen,
An Ate, stirring him to blood and strife;
With her her niece, the Lady Blanch of Spain;
With them a bastard of the king's deceased;
And all the unsettled humours of the land,
Rash, inconsiderate, fiery voluntaries,
With ladies' faces and fierce dragons' spleens,
Have sold their fortunes at their native homes,
Bearing their birthrights proudly on their backs,   70
To make a hazard of new fortunes here:
In brief, a braver choice of dauntless spirits
Than now the English bottoms have waft o'er
Did never float upon the swelling tide,
To do offence and scath in Christendom.   [Drum beats.
The interruption of their churlish drums
Cuts off more circumstance: they are at hand,
To parley or to fight; therefore prepare.
     K. PHI. How much unlook'd for is this expedition!
     AUST. By how much unexpected, by so much   80
We must awake endeavour for defence;
For courage mounteth with occasion:
Let them be welcome then; we are prepared.

---

60 *expedient*] expeditious, rapid.

63 *Ate*] The goddess of revenge or hate, belonging to Greek mythology.

64 *her niece, the Lady Blanch*] daughter of John's sister Elinor, who was married
     to Alphonso VIII, king of Castile; hence John's *niece* and his mother
     Queen Elinor's *granddaughter*.

65 *of the king's deceased*] of the deceased king's.

67 *voluntaries*] volunteers.

75 *scath*] harm, destruction; as in the modern "*scathe*-less."

77 *circumstance*] circumstantial detail.

Enter KING JOHN, ELINOR, BLANCH, *the* BASTARD, LORDS, *and Forces*

K. JOHN. Peace be to France, if France in peace permit
Our just and lineal entrance to our own;
If not, bleed France, and peace ascend to heaven,
Whiles we, God's wrathful agent, do correct
Their proud contempt that beats His peace to heaven.

K. PHI. Peace be to England, if that war return
From France to England, there to live in peace. 90
England we love; and for that England's sake
With burden of our armour here we sweat.
This toil of ours should be a work of thine;
But thou from loving England art so far,
That thou hast under-wrought his lawful king,
Cut off the sequence of posterity,
Out-faced infant state and done a rape
Upon the maiden virtue of the crown.
Look here upon thy brother Geffrey's face;
These eyes, these brows, were moulded out of his: 100
This little abstract doth contain that large
Which died in Geffrey, and the hand of time
Shall draw this brief into as huge a volume,
That Geffrey was thy elder brother born,
And this his son; England was Geffrey's right,
And this is Geffrey's: in the name of God
How comes it then that thou art call'd a king,
When living blood doth in these temples beat,
Which owe the crown that thou o'ermasterest?

K. JOHN. From whom hast thou this great commission, France, 110
To draw my answer from thy articles?

K. PHI. From that supernal judge, that stirs good thoughts
In any breast of strong authority,
To look into the blots and stains of right:
That judge hath made me guardian to this boy:
Under whose warrant I impeach thy wrong,

---

95 *under-wrought*] undermined, supplanted.
97 *Out-faced*] Insulted, brazenly affronted.
106 *this is Geffrey's*] The meaning is that this right to England (which Arthur
　　claims) is Geffrey's right (which Arthur inherits).
109 *owe*] own, possess.
114 *blots and stains*] an allusion to the heraldic signs of bastardy.

And by whose help I mean to chastise it.

    K. JOHN. Alack, thou dost usurp authority.

    K. PHI. Excuse; it is to beat usurping down.

    ELI. Who is it thou dost call usurper, France?   120

    CONST. Let me make answer; thy usurping son.

    ELI. Out, insolent! thy bastard shall be king,

That thou mayst be a queen, and check the world!

    CONST. My bed was ever to thy son as true

As thine was to thy husband; and this boy

Liker in feature to his father Geffrey

Than thou and John in manners; being as like

As rain to water, or devil to his dam.

My boy a bastard! By my soul, I think

His father never was so true begot: 130

It cannot be, an if thou wert his mother.

    ELI. There's a good mother, boy, that blots thy father.

    CONST. There's a good grandam, boy, that would blot thee.

    AUST. Peace!

    BAST.   Hear the crier.

    AUST.   What the devil art thou?

    BAST. One that will play the devil, sir, with you,

An a' may catch your hide and you alone:

You are the hare of whom the proverb goes,

Whose valour plucks dead lions by the beard:

I'll smoke your skin-coat, an I catch you right;

Sirrah, look to 't; i' faith, I will, i' faith.   140

    BLANCH. O, well did he become that lion's robe

That did disrobe the lion of that robe!

    BAST. It lies as sightly on the back of him

As great Alcides' shows upon an ass:

---

123 *a queen, and check the world*] an allusion to the queen's check in the game
of chess.

131 *an if thou wert his mother*] John's mother, Queen Elinor, had been divorced
for infidelity by her first husband Louis VII of France, before she married
Henry II of England.

134 *Hear the crier*] The crier was the official who proclaimed silence in courts
of justice. Austria has just cried "Peace!"

136 *your hide and you*] An allusion to the tradition that the Duke of Austria
robbed his prisoner Richard I of a lion's hide, which the duke thenceforth
himself wore.

139 *smoke your skin-coat*] beat your skin soundly.

144 *great Alcides'*] great Hercules' robe (made out of the skin of the Nemean lion).

But, ass, I'll take that burthen from your back,
Or lay on that shall make your shoulders crack.

AUST. What cracker is this same that deafs our ears
With this abundance of superfluous breath?
King Philip, determine what we shall do straight.

K. PHI. Women and fools, break off your conference. 150
King John, this is the very sum of all;
England and Ireland, Anjou, Touraine, Maine,
In right of Arthur do I claim of thee:
Wilt thou resign them and lay down thy arms?

K. JOHN. My life as soon: I do defy thee, France.
Arthur of Bretagne, yield thee to my hand;
And out of my dear love I'll give thee more
Than e'er the coward hand of France can win:
Submit thee, boy.

ELI.   Come to thy grandam, child.

CONST. Do, child, go to it grandam, child; 160
Give grandam kingdom, and it grandam will
Give it a plum, a cherry, and a fig:
There's a good grandam.

ARTH.   Good my mother, peace!
I would that I were low laid in my grave:
I am not worth this coil that's made for me.

ELI. His mother shames him so, poor boy, he weeps.

CONST. Now shame upon you, whether she does or no!
His grandam's wrongs, and not his mother's shames,
Draws those heaven-moving pearls from his poor eyes,
Which heaven shall take in nature of a fee; 170
Ay, with these crystal beads heaven shall be bribed
To do him justice and revenge on you.

ELI. Thou monstrous slanderer of heaven and earth!

CONST. Thou monstrous injurer of heaven and earth!
Call not me slanderer; thou and thine usurp

---

147 *cracker*] braggart.
160 *it grandam*] its grandam.
165 *coil*] fuss, commotion.
168 *His grandam's wrongs*] Wrongs done by his grandam.

The dominations, royalties and rights
Of this oppressed boy: this is thy eld'st son's son,
Infortunate in nothing but in thee:
Thy sins are visited in this poor child;
The canon of the law is laid on him,   180
Being but the second generation
Removed from thy sin-conceiving womb.

    K. JOHN. Bedlam, have done.

    CONST.   I have but this to say,
That he is not only plagued for her sin,
But God hath made her sin and her the plague
On this removed issue, plagued for her
And with her plague; her sin his injury,
Her injury the beadle to her sin,
All punish'd in the person of this child,
And all for her; a plague upon her!   190

    ELI. Thou unadvised scold, I can produce
A will that bars the title of thy son.

    CONST. Ay, who doubts that? a will! a wicked will;
A woman's will; a canker'd grandam's will!

    K. PHI. Peace, lady! pause, or be more temperate:
It ill beseems this presence to cry aim
To these ill-tuned repetitions.
Some trumpet summon hither to the walls
These men of Angiers: let us hear them speak
Whose title they admit, Arthur's or John's.   200

---

180 *The canon of the law*] The sins of fathers shall be visited on the children
"unto the third and fourth generation" according to the Jewish law re-
corded in Exodus xx, 5.

183 *Bedlam*] woman of the madhouse, *i.e.*, Bedlam or Bethlehem hospital.

185–189 *But God hath made … of this child*] God hath made her sin and herself
alike a curse on this distant kinsman of hers, who is afflicted both by the
punishment allotted her, and also by the punishment which she inflicts on
him; her sin brings Arthur injury; her injurious conduct inflicts on the boy
(like a beadle who punishes youthful offenders) the punishment incurred
by her offence. Arthur is in every way her scapegoat.

191 *unadvised*] rash.

196 *cry aim*] give encouragement; a term in archery applied to those who stand
by the archer bidding him to what point to direct his aim.

Trumpet sounds. Enter certain CITIZENS *upon the walls*

FIRST CIT. Who is it that hath warn'd us to the walls?

K. PHI. 'T is France, for England.

K. JOHN.   England, for itself.

You men of Angiers, and my loving subjects,—

K. PHI. You loving men of Angiers, Arthur's subjects,

Our trumpet call'd you to this gentle parle,—

K. JOHN. For our advantage; therefore hear us first.

These flags of France, that are advanced here

Before the eye and prospect of your town,

Have hither march'd to your endamagement:

The cannons have their bowels full of wrath,   210

And ready mounted are they to spit forth

Their iron indignation 'gainst your walls:

All preparation for a bloody siege

And merciless proceeding by these French

Confronts your city's eyes, your winking gates;

And but for our approach those sleeping stones,

That as a waist doth girdle you about,

By the compulsion of their ordinance

By this time from their fixed beds of lime

Had been dishabited, and wide havoc made   220

For bloody power to rush upon your peace.

But on the sight of us your lawful king,

Who painfully with much expedient march

Have brought a countercheck before your gates,

To save unscratch'd your city's threatened cheeks,

Behold, the French amazed vouchsafe a parle;

And now, instead of bullets wrapp'd in fire,

To make a shaking fever in your walls,

They shoot but calm words folded up in smoke,

To make a faithless error in your ears: 230

Which trust accordingly, kind citizens,

---

209 *endamagement*] loss.

215 *winking*] closed (in sleep).

218 *ordinance*] ordnance, artillery.

220 *dishabited*] dislodged.

223 *expedient*] expeditious, rapid.

230 *To make ... in your ears*] To cause you to be deceived, to lead you into an error of disloyalty.

And let us in, your king, whose labour'd spirits,
Forwearied in this action of swift speed,
Crave harbourage within your city walls.
     K. PHI. When I have said, make answer to us both.
Lo, in this right hand, whose protection
Is most divinely vow'd upon the right
Of him it holds, stands young Plantagenet,
Son to the elder brother of this man,
And king o'er him and all that he enjoys: 240
For this down-trodden equity, we tread
In warlike march these greens before your town,
Being no further enemy to you
Than the constraint of hospitable zeal
In the relief of this oppressed child
Religiously provokes. Be pleased then
To pay that duty which you truly owe
To him that owes it, namely this young prince:
And then our arms, like to a muzzled bear,
Save in aspect, hath all offence seal'd up;   250
Our cannons' malice vainly shall be spent
Against the invulnerable clouds of heaven;
And with a blessed and unvex'd retire,
With unhack'd swords and helmets all unbruised,
We will bear home that lusty blood again,
Which here we came to spout against your town,
And leave your children, wives and you in peace.
But if you fondly pass our proffer'd offer,
'T is not the roundure of your old-faced walls
Can hide you from our messengers of war,   260
Though all these English and their discipline
Were harbour'd in their rude circumference.
Then tell us, shall your city call us lord,
In that behalf which we have challenged it?
Or shall we give the signal to our rage
And stalk in blood to our possession?

---

233 *Forwearied*] Outwearied, worn out.
242 *greens*] meadows.
247–248 *owe ... owes*] "owe" is first used here in its ordinary modern sense,
    and then in its old sense of "own."
253 *retire*] withdrawal, retreat.
259 *roundure*] round, circle.

First Cit. In brief, we are the king of England's subjects:
For him, and in his right, we hold this town.

K. John. Acknowledge then the king, and let me in.

First Cit. That can we not; but he that proves the king,
To him will we prove loyal: till that time
Have we ramm'd up our gates against the world.

K. John. Doth not the crown of England prove the king?　270
And if not that, I bring you witnesses,
Twice fifteen thousand hearts of England's breed,—

Bast. Bastards, and else.

K. John. To verify our title with their lives.

K. Phi. As many and as well-born bloods as those—

Bast. Some bastards too.

K. Phi. Stand in his face to contradict his claim.　280

First Cit. Till you compound whose right is worthiest,
We for the worthiest hold the right from both.

K. John. Then God forgive the sin of all those souls
That to their everlasting residence,
Before the dew of evening fall, shall fleet,
In dreadful trial of our kingdom's king!

K. Phi. Amen, amen! Mount, chevaliers! to arms!

Bast. Saint George, that swinged the dragon, and e'er since
Sits on his horse back at mine hostess' door,
Teach us some fence! [*To Aust.*] Sirrah, were I at home,　290
At your den, sirrah, with your lioness,
I would set an ox-head to your lion's hide,
And make a monster of you.

Aust.　　　　　　　　　Peace! no more.

Bast. O, tremble, for you hear the lion roar.

K. John. Up higher to the plain; where we'll set forth
In best appointment all our regiments.

Bast. Speed then, to take advantage of the field.

K. Phi. It shall be so; and at the other hill
Command the rest to stand. God and our right!

　　　　　　　　　　　　　　　　　　　　[Exeunt.

---

272 *ramm'd up*] closed by means of wedges driven into the apertures by battering-
　rams.

278 *bloods*] men of spirit, gallants.

288–289 *Saint George ... at mine hostess' door*] St. George and the dragon was a
　very common tavern sign.

Here after excursions, enter the Herald of France, *with trumpets,*
to the gates

F. HER. You men of Angiers, open wide your gates,   300
And let young Arthur, Duke of Bretagne, in,
Who by the hand of France this day hath made
Much work for tears in many an English mother,
Whose sons lie scattered on the bleeding ground:
Many a widow's husband grovelling lies,
Coldly embracing the discoloured earth;
And victory, with little loss, doth play
Upon the dancing banners of the French,
Who are at hand, triumphantly display'd,
To enter conquerors, and to proclaim   310
Arthur of Bretagne England's king and yours.

Enter English Herald, *with trumpet*

E. HER. Rejoice, you men of Angiers, ring your bells;
King John, your king and England's, doth approach,
Commander of this hot malicious day:
Their armours, that march'd hence so silver-bright,
Hither return all gilt with Frenchmen's blood;
There stuck no plume in any English crest
That is removed by a staff of France;
Our colours do return in those same hands
That did display them when we first march'd forth;   320
And, like a jolly troop of huntsmen, come
Our lusty English, all with purpled hands,
Dyed in the dying slaughter of their foes:
Open your gates and give the victors way.

FIRST CIT. Heralds, from off our towers we might behold,
From first to last, the onset and retire
Of both your armies; whose equality
By our best eyes cannot be censured:
Blood hath bought blood and blows have answered blows;

---

314 *hot*] hotly (or fiercely) contested (or fought).

322 *with purpled hands*] Hunters (of deer) in Elizabethan England dipped their
    hands in the blood of their quarry when it was killed.

326 *retire*] retreat.

327–328 *whose equality … censured*] whose evenness of power will not permit
    the best eyes to estimate which is superior.

Strength match'd with strength, and power confronted power: 330
Both are alike; and both alike we like.
One must prove greatest: while they weigh so even,
We hold our town for neither, yet for both.

Re-enter the two KINGS, *with their powers, severally*

K. JOHN. France, hast thou yet more blood to cast away?
Say, shall the current of our right run on?
Whose passage, vex'd with thy impediment,
Shall leave his native channel, and o'erswell
With course disturb'd even thy confining shores,
Unless thou let his silver water keep
A peaceful progress to the ocean.   340
     K. PHI. England, thou hast not saved one drop of blood,
In this hot trial, more than we of France;
Rather, lost more. And by this hand I swear,
That sways the earth this climate overlooks,
Before we will lay down our just-borne arms,
We'll put thee down, 'gainst whom these arms we bear,
Or add a royal number to the dead,
Gracing the scroll that tells of this war's loss
With slaughter coupled to the name of kings.
     BAST. Ha, majesty! how high thy glory towers,   350
When the rich blood of kings is set on fire!
O, now doth Death line his dead chaps with steel;
The swords of soldiers are his teeth, his fangs;
And now he feasts, mousing the flesh of men,
In undetermined differences of kings.
Why stand these royal fronts amazed thus?
Cry "havoc!" kings; back to the stained field,
You equal potents, fiery kindled spirits!
Then let confusion of one part confirm

---

344 *this climate overlooks*] which the region of the heavens immediately above
   us overlooks.
347 *add a royal number to the dead*] add a king to the number of the dead.
354 *mousing*] devouring (as the cat eats the mouse).
356 *fronts*] brows.
357 *Cry "havoc"*] The cry which gave the signal for "no quarter."
358 *equal potents*] evenly matched potentates, powers.
359 *confusion of one part*] ruin of one side.

The other's peace; till then, blows, blood, and death!   360
   K. JOHN. Whose party do the townsmen yet admit?
   K. PHI. Speak, citizens, for England; who's your king?
   FIRST CIT. The king of England, when we know the king.
   K. PHI. Know him in us, that here hold up his right.
   K. JOHN. In us, that are our own great deputy,
And bear possession of our person here,
Lord of our presence, Angiers, and of you.
   FIRST CIT. A greater power than we denies all this;
And till it be undoubted, we do lock
Our former scruple in our strong-barr'd gates;   370
King'd of our fears, until our fears, resolved,
Be by some certain king purged and deposed.
   BAST. By heaven, these scroyles of Angiers flout you, kings,
And stand securely on their battlements,
As in a theatre, whence they gape and point
At your industrious scenes and acts of death.
Your royal presences be ruled by me:
Do like the mutines of Jerusalem,
Be friends awhile and both conjointly bend
Your sharpest deeds of malice on this town: 380
By east and west let France and England mount
Their battering cannon charged to the mouths,
Till their soul-fearing clamours have brawl'd down
The flinty ribs of this contemptuous city:
I'ld play incessantly upon these jades,
Even till unfenced desolation
Leave them as naked as the vulgar air.
That done, dissever your united strengths,
And part your mingled colours once again;
Turn face to face and bloody point to point;   390
Then, in a moment, Fortune shall cull forth

---

367 *Lord of our presence*] Lord of our person.
368 *A greater power*] Providence.
371 *King'd of our fears*] Ruled by our fears.
373 *scroyles*] scrofulous fellows; from the French "escrouelles" (*i.e.*, vermin).
378 *the mutines of Jerusalem*] The mutineers of Jerusalem. A reference to two
    Jewish chiefs—at the head of two warring factions—who sank their differ-
    ences to unite their forces against Titus when he besieged Jerusalem.
383 *soul-fearing*] soul-appalling.
385 *jades*] vicious creatures; applied to vicious horses and mares alike.

Out of one side her happy minion,
To whom in favour she shall give the day,
And kiss him with a glorious victory.
How like you this wild counsel, mighty states?
Smacks it not something of the policy?

    K. JOHN. Now, by the sky that hangs above our heads,
I like it well. France, shall we knit our powers
And lay this Angiers even with the ground;
Then after fight who shall be king of it?   400

    BAST. An if thou hast the mettle of a king,
Being wrong'd as we are by this peevish town,
Turn thou the mouth of thy artillery,
As we will ours, against these saucy walls;
And when that we have dash'd them to the ground,
Why then defy each other, and pell-mell
Make work upon ourselves, for heaven or hell.

    K. PHI. Let it be so. Say, where will you assault?

    K. JOHN. We from the west will send destruction
Into this city's bosom.   410

    AUST. I from the north.

    K. PHI.   Our thunder from the south
Shall rain their drift of bullets on this town.

    BAST. O prudent discipline! From north to south:
Austria and France shoot in each other's mouth:
I'll stir them to it. Come, away, away!

    FIRST CIT. Hear us, great kings: vouchsafe awhile to stay,
And I shall show you peace and fair-faced league;
Win you this city without stroke or wound;
Rescue those breathing lives to die in beds,
That here come sacrifices for the field: 420
Persever not, but hear me, mighty kings.

    K. JOHN. Speak on with favour; we are bent to hear.

    FIRST CIT. That daughter there of Spain, the Lady Blanch,
Is niece to England: look upon the years
Of Lewis the Dauphin and that lovely maid:
If lusty love should go in quest of beauty,

---

392 *minion*] favourite.
393 *mighty states*] mighty rulers of states, princes.
402 *peevish*] wayward, petulant.
411–412 *Our thunder … drift*] Our thundering cannon shall hurl their driving
    shower.

Where should he find it fairer than in Blanch?
If zealous love should go in search of virtue,
Where should he find it purer than in Blanch?
If love ambitious sought a match of birth,
Whose veins bound richer blood than Lady Blanch?
Such as she is, in beauty, virtue, birth,   430
Is the young Dauphin every way complete:
If not complete of, say he is not she;
And she again wants nothing, to name want,
If want it be not that she is not he:
He is the half part of a blessed man,
Left to be finished by such as she;
And she a fair divided excellence,
Whose fulness of perfection lies in him.   440
O, two such silver currents, when they join,
Do glorify the banks that bound them in;
And two such shores to two such streams made one,
Two such controlling bounds shall you be, kings,
To these two princes, if you marry them.
This union shall do more than battery can
To our fast-closed gates; for at this match,
With swifter spleen than powder can enforce,
The mouth of passage shall we fling wide ope,
And give you entrance: but without this match,   450
The sea enraged is not half so deaf,
Lions more confident, mountains and rocks
More free from motion, no, not Death himself
In mortal fury half so peremptory,
As we to keep this city.
    BAST.   Here's a stay
That shakes the rotten carcass of old Death
Out of his rags! Here's a large mouth, indeed,
That spits forth death and mountains, rocks and seas,
Talks as familiarly of roaring lions

---

434 *complete of*] full of (these virtues).
435–436 *to name want ... she is not he*] to use so inappropriate a word as "want"
    in this connection, unless we treat it as a want that she is not he.
448 *spleen*] eagerness, impetuous haste.
452–453 *Lions more confident ... More free*] The negative of line 460 is implied
    in both clauses, *i.e.,* Lions are *not* more confident, etc.
455 *a stay*] a barrier, an obstacle, a check.

As maids of thirteen do of puppy-dogs! 460
What cannoneer begot this lusty blood?
He speaks plain cannon fire, and smoke and bounce;
He gives the bastinado with his tongue:
Our ears are cudgell'd; not a word of his
But buffets better than a fist of France:
Zounds! I was never so bethump'd with words
Since I first call'd my brother's father dad.

ELI. Son, list to this conjunction, make this match;
Give with our niece a dowry large enough:
For by this knot thou shalt so surely tie 470
Thy now unsured assurance to the crown,
That yon green boy shall have no sun to ripe
The bloom that promiseth a mighty fruit.
I see a yielding in the looks of France;
Mark, how they whisper: urge them while their souls
Are capable of this ambition,
Lest zeal, now melted by the windy breath
Of soft petitions, pity and remorse,
Cool and congeal again to what it was.

FIRST CIT. Why answer not the double majesties 480
This friendly treaty of our threaten'd town?

K. PHI. Speak England first, that hath been forward first
To speak unto this city: what say you?

K. JOHN. If that the Dauphin there, thy princely son,
Can in this book of beauty read "I love,"
Her dowry shall weigh equal with a queen:
For Anjou, and fair Touraine, Maine, Poictiers,
And all that we upon this side the sea,
Except this city now by us besieged,
Find liable to our crown and dignity, 490
Shall gild her bridal bed, and make her rich

---

461 *blood*] gallant.
462 *bounce*] report or bang of a gun.
463 *the bastinado*] a sound thrashing.
468 *conjunction*] matrimonial union.
471 *unsured*] uncertain.
477–479 *zeal ... Cool and congeal again*] The present zeal (in the previously hard
    heart of King Philip) is compared to melted ice, and the fear is expressed
    that it may freeze to ice again.
478 *remorse*] compassion.

In titles, honours and promotions,
As she in beauty, education, blood,
Holds hand with any princess of the world.

    K. Phi. What say'st thou, boy? look in the lady's face.

    Lew. I do, my lord; and in her eye I find
A wonder, or a wondrous miracle,
The shadow of myself form'd in her eye;
Which, being but the shadow of your son,
Becomes a sun and makes your son a shadow: 500
I do protest I never loved myself
Till now infixed I beheld myself
Drawn in the flattering table of her eye.

                           [*Whispers with Blanch.*

    Bast. Drawn in the flattering table of her eye!
        Hang'd in the frowning wrinkle of her brow!
And quarter'd in her heart! he doth espy
        Himself love's traitor: this is pity now,
That, hang'd and drawn and quarter'd there should be,
In such a love so vile a lout as he.

    Blanch. My uncle's will in this respect is mine: 510
If he see aught in you that makes him like,
That any thing he sees, which moves his liking,
I can with ease translate it to my will;
Or if you will, to speak more properly,
I will enforce it easily to my love.
Further I will not flatter you, my lord,
That all I see in you is worthy love,
Than this; that nothing do I see in you,
Though churlish thoughts themselves should be your judge,
That I can find should merit any hate.   520

    K. John. What say these young ones? What say you, my niece?

    Blanch. That she is bound in honour still to do
What you in wisdom still vouchsafe to say.

    K. John. Speak then, prince Dauphin; can you love this lady?

    Lew. Nay, ask me if I can refrain from love;

---

503 *table*] canvas or board (on which a picture is painted).

504–509 *Drawn ... as he*] This speech is in the six-line stanza of *Venus and Adonis.*

504–506 *Drawn ... Hang'd ... quarter'd*] A reference to the three stages of punishment inflicted on traitors who were first drawn to the gallows on a hurdle, then hanged, then hewn into quarters.

For I do love her most unfeignedly.

    K. JOHN. Then do I give Volquessen, Touraine, Maine,
Poictiers, and Anjou, these five provinces,
With her to thee; and this addition more,
Full thirty thousand marks of English coin.   530
Philip of France, if thou be pleased withal,
Command thy son and daughter to join hands.

    K. PHI. It likes us well; young princes, close your hands.

    AUST. And your lips too; for I am well assured
That I did so when I was first assured.

    K. PHI. Now, citizens of Angiers, ope your gates,
Let in that amity which you have made;
For at Saint Mary's chapel presently
The rites of marriage shall be solemnized.
Is not the Lady Constance in this troop?   540
I know she is not, for this match made up
Her presence would have interrupted much:
Where is she and her son? tell me, who knows.

    LEW. She is sad and passionate at your highness' tent.

    K. PHI. And, by my faith, this league that we have made
Will give her sadness very little cure.
Brother of England, how may we content
This widow lady? In her right we came;
Which we, God knows, have turn'd another way,
To our own vantage.

    K. JOHN.   We will heal up all;   550
For we'll create young Arthur Duke of Bretagne
And Earl of Richmond; and this rich fair town
We make him lord of. Call the Lady Constance;
Some speedy messenger bid her repair
To our solemnity: I trust we shall,
If not fill up the measure of her will,
Yet in some measure satisfy her so
That we shall stop her exclamation.
Go we, as well as haste will suffer us,
To this unlook'd for, unprepared pomp.   560

                [*Exeunt all but the Bastard.*

---

527 *Volquessen*] The ancient name *(Pagus Velocessinus)* of the Vexin, the district
    round Rouen.

535 *first assured*] first affianced, betrothed.

544 *passionate*] agitated (by passion).

BAST. Mad world! mad kings! mad composition!
John, to stop Arthur's title in the whole,
Hath willingly departed with a part:
And France, whose armour conscience buckled on,
Whom zeal and charity brought to the field
As God's own soldier, rounded in the ear
With that same purpose-changer, that sly devil,
That broker, that still breaks the pate of faith,
That daily break-vow, he that wins of all,
Of kings, of beggars, old men, young men, maids,   570
Who, having no external thing to lose
But the word "maid," cheats the poor maid of that,
That smooth-faced gentleman, tickling Commodity,
Commodity, the bias of the world,
The world, who of itself is peised well.
Made to run even upon even ground,
Till this advantage, this vile-drawing bias,
This sway of motion, this Commodity,
Makes it take head from all indifferency,
From all direction, purpose, course, intent: 580
And this same bias, this Commodity,
This bawd, this broker, this all-changing word,
Clapp'd on the outward eye of fickle France,
Hath drawn him from his own determined aid,
From a resolved and honourable war,
To a most base and vile-concluded peace.
And why rail I on this Commodity?
But for because he hath not woo'd me yet:

---

561 *composition*] compact, treaty.
563 *departed*] parted.
566 *rounded*] whispered.
571–572 *having* ... "*maid*"] this is an absolute clause, with an implied subject "they" (*i.e.,* "maids") which governs "having."
573 *tickling* ... *Commodity*] flattering, cajoling, ... Self-interest or Expediency.
574 *the bias*] Literally the piece of lead fixed to a bowl to make it swerve when played in the game. "Commodity" is here defined as an influence making the world swerve from its right course.
575 *who* ... *is peised*] which is poised or balanced.
579 *Makes it take* ... *indifferency*] Makes it deviate altogether from the direction of impartiality or judicial equity.
582 *broker*] go-between, pimp.
584 *his own determined aid*] the aid he had determined to give.

Not that I have the power to clutch my hand,
When his fair angels would salute my palm;   590
But for my hand, as unattempted yet,
Like a poor beggar, raileth on the rich,
Well, whiles I am a beggar, I will rail
And say there is no sin but to be rich;
And being rich, my virtue then shall be
To say there is no vice but beggary.
Since kings break faith upon commodity,
Gain, be my lord, for I will worship thee.   [*Exit.*

---

589 *clutch*] clench, shut.
590 *angels*] gold coins, worth about ten shillings apiece.

ACT III.
SCENE I. *The French King's Pavilion.*

Enter CONSTANCE, ARTHUR, *and* SALISBURY

CONSTANCE. Gone to be married! gone to swear a peace!
False blood to false blood join'd! gone to be friends!
Shall Lewis have Blanch, and Blanch those provinces?
It is not so; thou hast misspoke, misheard;
Be well advised, tell o'er thy tale again:
It cannot be; thou dost but say 't is so:
I trust I may not trust thee; for thy word
Is but the vain breath of a common man:
Believe me, I do not believe thee, man;
I have a king's oath to the contrary.   10
Thou shalt be punish'd for thus frighting me,
For I am sick and capable of fears,
Oppress'd with wrongs and therefore full of fears,
A widow, husbandless, subject to fears,
A woman, naturally born to fears;
And though thou now confess thou didst but jest,
With my vex'd spirits I cannot take a truce,
But they will quake and tremble all this day.
What dost thou mean by shaking of thy head?
Why dost thou look so sadly on my son?   20
What means that hand upon that breast of thine?
Why holds thine eye that lamentable rheum,
Like a proud river peering o'er his bounds?
Be these sad signs confirmers of thy words?
Then speak again; not all thy former tale,
But this one word, whether thy tale be true.

SAL. As true as I believe you think them false
That give you cause to prove my saying true.

---

14 *A widow*] As a matter of history, Constance was at this period wife of a third
   husband, Guy, Count of Thouars. After the death of Prince Arthur's father, Geffrey (her first husband), she married, secondly, Randolph de
   Blundeville, Earl of Chester, whom she divorced.

22 *lamentable rheum*] tears of sorrow or lamentation.

24 *these sad signs*] the shaking of the head, the laying of the hand on the breast,
   the tearful eye, to which the speaker has just drawn attention.

CONST. O, if thou teach me to believe this sorrow,
Teach thou this sorrow how to make me die,   30
And let belief and life encounter so
As doth the fury of two desperate men
Which in the very meeting fall and die.
Lewis marry Blanch! O boy, then where art thou?
France friend with England, what becomes of me?
Fellow, be gone: I cannot brook thy sight:
This news hath made thee a most ugly man.
     SAL. What other harm have I, good lady, done,
But spoke the harm that is by others done?
     CONST. Which harm within itself so heinous is   40
As it makes harmful all that speak of it.
     ARTH. I do beseech you, madam, be content.
     CONST. If thou, that bid'st me be content, wert grim,
Ugly and slanderous to thy mother's womb,
Full of unpleasing blots and sightless stains,
Lame, foolish, crooked, swart, prodigious,
Patch'd with foul moles and eye-offending marks,
I would not care, I then would be content,
For then I should not love thee, no, nor thou
Become thy great birth nor deserve a crown.   50
But thou art fair, and at thy birth, dear boy,
Nature and Fortune join'd to make thee great:
Of Nature's gifts thou mayst with lilies boast
And with the half-blown rose. But Fortune, O,
She is corrupted, changed and won from thee;
She adulterates hourly with thine uncle John,
And with her golden hand hath pluck'd on France
To tread down fair respect of sovereignty,
And made his majesty the bawd to theirs.
France is a bawd to Fortune and King John,   60
That strumpet Fortune, that usurping John!
Tell me, thou fellow, is not France forsworn?
Envenom him with words, or get thee gone,
And leave those woes alone which I alone

---

45 *blots ... stains*] "Sightless" means "unsightly."
46 *swart, prodigious*] ill-favouredly dark, monstrously misshapen.
56 *adulterates*] commits adultery.
63 *Envenom*] Poison.

Am bound to under-bear.

    SAL.   Pardon me, madam,
I may not go without you to the kings.

    CONST. Thou mayst, thou shalt; I will not go with thee:
I will instruct my sorrows to be proud;
For grief is proud and makes his owner stoop.
To me and to the state of my great grief   70
Let kings assemble; for my grief's so great
That no supporter but the huge firm earth
Can hold it up: here I and sorrows sit;
Here is my throne, bid kings come bow to it.

                                [*Seats herself on the ground.*

    Enter KING JOHN, KING PHILIP, LEWIS, BLANCH, ELINOR, *the*
                    BASTARD, AUSTRIA, *and* Attendants

    K. PHI. 'T is true, fair daughter; and this blessed day
Ever in France shall be kept festival:
To solemnize this day the glorious sun
Stays in his course and plays the alchemist,
Turning with spendour of his precious eye
The meagre cloddy earth to glittering gold: 80
The yearly course that brings this day about
Shall never see it but a holiday.

    CONST. A wicked day, and not a holy day!   [*Rising.*
What hath this day deserved? what hath it done,
That it in golden letters should be set
Among the high tides in the calendar?
Nay, rather turn this day out of the week,
This day of shame, oppression, perjury.
Or, if it must stand still, let wives with child,
Pray that their burthens may not fall this day,   90
Lest that their hopes prodigiously be cross'd:

---

69 *stoop*] Constance is too agitated to make her imagery quite consistent. She
    means that she is prostrated to the ground by the weight of her grief: she
    will not obey the summons of the kings; they must come to her and bow
    down before her who lies prone on the earth.
86 *high tides*] days of high festivals, solemn seasons.
91 *prodigiously be cross'd*] be frustrated by misshapen abortions.

But on this day let seamen fear no wreck;
No bargains break that are not this day made:
This day, all things begun come to ill end,
Yea, faith itself to hollow falsehood change!

K. PHI. By heaven, lady, you shall have no cause
To curse the fair proceedings of this day:
Have I not pawn'd to you my majesty?

CONST. You have beguiled me with a counterfeit
Resembling majesty, which, being touch'd and tried,   100
Proves valueless: you are forsworn, forsworn;
You came in arms to spill mine enemies' blood,
But now in arms you strengthen it with yours:
The grappling vigour and rough frown of war
Is cold in amity and painted peace,
And our oppression hath made up this league.
Arm, arm, you heavens, against these perjured kings!
A widow cries; be husband to me, heavens!
Let not the hours of this ungodly day
Wear out the day in peace; but, ere sunset,   110
Set armed discord 'twixt these perjured kings!
Hear me, O, hear me!

AUST.   Lady Constance, peace!

CONST. War! war! no peace! peace is to me a war.
O Lymoges! O Austria! thou dost shame
That bloody spoil: thou slave, thou wretch, thou coward!
Thou little valiant, great in villany!
Thou ever strong upon the stronger side!
Thou Fortune's champion, that dost never fight
But when her humorous ladyship is by
To teach thee safety! thou art perjured too,   120
And soothest up greatness. What a fool art thou,

---

92 *But on this day*] Except on this day, on this day only.
99 *counterfeit*] base coin.
100 *touch'd and tried*] tested by the touchstone.
103 *now in arms ... with yours*] now in embraces you support my enemies with
     your blood.
105 *painted peace*] pretence of peace.
114 *O Lymoges! O Austria!*] Titles of two quite different persons, who are
     confused together.
121 *soothest up*] flatterest up.

A ramping fool, to brag and stamp and swear
Upon my party! Thou cold-blooded slave,
Hast thou not spoke like thunder on my side,
Been sworn my soldier, bidding me depend
Upon thy stars, thy fortune and thy strength,
And dost thou now fall over to my foes?
Thou wear a lion's hide! doff it for shame,
And hang a calf's-skin on those recreant limbs.

    AUST. O, that a man should speak those words to me!   130
    BAST. And hang a calf's-skin on those recreant limbs.
    AUST. Thou darest not say so, villain, for thy life.
    BAST. And hang a calf's-skin on those recreant limbs.
    K. JOHN. We like not this; thou dost forget thyself.

Enter PANDULPH

    K. PHI. Here comes the holy legate of the pope.
    PAND. Hail, you anointed deputies of heaven!
To thee, King John, my holy errand is.
I Pandulph, of fair Milan cardinal,
And from Pope Innocent the legate here,
Do in his name religiously demand   140
Why thou against the church, our holy mother,
So wilfully dost spurn; and force perforce
Keep Stephen Langton, chosen archbishop
Of Canterbury, from that holy see:
This, in our foresaid holy father's name,
Pope Innocent, I do demand of thee.
    K. JOHN. What earthy name to interrogatories
Can task the free breath of a sacred king?

---

122 *ramping*] gesticulating with violence; used of rearing horses.
123 *Upon my party*] Against my side.
127 *fall over*] go over, revolt.
129 *a calf's-skin*] a fool's coat.
142 *force perforce*] willy-nilly, in despite of everything.
147–148 *What earthy name ... sacred king*] What earthly name or power can
    coerce or compel the free speech of a sacred king to reply to interrogato-
    ries (*i.e.*, formal questions in legal procedure which have to be answered
    on oath).

Thou canst not, cardinal, devise a name
So slight, unworthy and ridiculous, 150
To charge me to an answer, as the pope.
Tell him this tale; and from the mouth of England
Add thus much more, that no Italian priest
Shall tithe or toll in our dominions;
But as we, under heaven, are supreme head,
So under Him that great supremacy,
Where we do reign, we will alone uphold,
Without the assistance of a mortal hand.
So tell the pope, all reverence set apart
To him and his usurp'd authority. 160
    K. PHI. Brother of England, you blaspheme in this.
    K. JOHN. Though you and all the kings of Christendom
Are led so grossly by this meddling priest,
Dreading the curse that money may buy out;
And by the merit of vile gold, dross, dust,
Purchase corrupted pardon of a man,
Who in that sale sells pardon from himself,
Though you and all the rest so grossly led
This juggling witchcraft with revenue cherish,
Yet I alone, alone do me oppose 170
Against the pope and count his friends my foes.
    PAND. Then, by the lawful power that I have,
Thou shalt stand cursed and excommunicate:
And blessed shall he be that doth revolt
From his allegiance to an heretic;
And meritorious shall that hand be call'd,
Canonized and worshipp'd as a saint,
That takes away by any secret course
Thy hateful life.
    CONST.   O, lawful let it be
That I have room with Rome to curse awhile! 180
Good father cardinal, cry thou amen
To my keen curses; for without my wrong
There is no tongue hath power to curse him right.
    PAND. There's law and warrant, lady, for my curse.
    CONST. And for mine too: when law can do no right,

---

154 *Shall tithe or toll*] Shall take tithe or levy tax.
159–160 *all reverence ... To him*] all respect for him being revoked.

Let it be lawful that law bar no wrong:
Law cannot give my child his kingdom here,
For he that holds his kingdom holds the law;
Therefore, since law itself is perfect wrong,
How can the law forbid my tongue to curse?   190

PAND. Philip of France, on peril of a curse,
Let go the hand of that arch-heretic;
And raise the power of France upon his head,
Unless he do submit himself to Rome.

ELI. Look'st thou pale, France? do not let go thy hand.

CONST. Look to that, devil; lest that France repent,
And by disjoining hands, hell lose a soul.

AUST. King Philip, listen to the cardinal.

BAST. And hang a calf's-skin on his recreant limbs.

AUST. Well, ruffian, I must pocket up these wrongs,   200
Because—

BAST. Your breeches best may carry them.

K. JOHN. Philip, what say'st thou to the cardinal?

CONST. What should he say, but as the cardinal?

LEW. Bethink you, father; for the difference
Is purchase of a heavy curse from Rome,
Or the light loss of England for a friend:
Forgo the easier.

BLANCH.   That's the curse of Rome.

CONST. O Lewis, stand fast! the devil tempts thee here
In likeness of a new untrimmed bride.   210

BLANCH. The Lady Constance speaks not from her faith,
But from her need.

CONST.   O, if thou grant my need,
Which only lives but by the death of faith,
That need must needs infer this principle,
That faith would live again by death of need.
O then, tread down my need, and faith mounts up;
Keep my need up, and faith is trodden down!

K. JOHN. The king is moved, and answers not to this.

CONST. O, be removed from him, and answer well!

AUST. Do so, King Philip; hang no more in doubt.   220

BAST. Hang nothing but a calf's-skin, most sweet lout.

---

210 *untrimmed bride*] bride undrest for the nuptial couch. "Untrimmed" is also
found in the sense of "with hair hanging loose."
214 *infer*] prove.

K. PHI. I am perplex'd, and know not what to say.

PAND. What canst thou say but will perplex thee more,
If thou stand excommunicate and cursed?

K. PHI. Good reverend father, make my person yours,
And tell me how you would bestow yourself.
This royal hand and mine are newly knit,
And the conjunction of our inward souls
Married in league, coupled and link'd together
With all religious strength of sacred vows;   230
The latest breath that gave the sound of words
Was deep-sworn faith, peace, amity, true love
Between our kingdoms and our royal selves,
And even before this truce, but new before,
No longer than we well could wash our hands
To clap this royal bargain up of peace,
Heaven knows, they were besmear'd and overstain'd
With slaughter's pencil, where revenge did paint
The fearful difference of incensed kings:
And shall these hands, so lately purged of blood,   240
So newly join'd in love, so strong in both,
Unyoke this seizure and this kind regreet?
Play fast and loose with faith? so jest with heaven,
Make such unconstant children of ourselves,
As now again to snatch our palm from palm,
Unswear faith sworn, and on the marriage-bed
Of smiling peace to march a bloody host,
And make a riot on the gentle brow
Of true sincerity? O, holy sir,
My reverend father, let it not be so!   250
Out of your grace, devise, ordain, impose
Some gentle order; and then we shall be blest
To do your pleasure and continue friends.

PAND. All form is formless, order orderless,
Save what is opposite to England's love.
Therefore to arms! be champion of our church,

---

226 *bestow yourself*] proceed to act.
236 *clap ... up*] clinch by striking or shaking hands.
241 *so strong in both*] deeds of blood and deeds of love.
242 *regreet*] salutation.
243 *fast and loose*] the name of a popular cheating game.
255 *opposite*] hostile, adverse.

Or let the church, our mother, breathe her curse,
A mother's curse, on her revolting son.
France, thou mayst hold a serpent by the tongue,
A chafed lion by the mortal paw,   260
A fasting tiger safer by the tooth,
Than keep in peace that hand which thou dost hold.
    K. PHI. I may disjoin my hand, but not my faith.
    PAND. So makest thou faith an enemy to faith;
And like a civil war set'st oath to oath,
Thy tongue against thy tongue. O, let thy vow
First made to heaven, first be to heaven perform'd,
That is, to be the champion of our church.
What since thou sworest is sworn against thyself
And may not be performed by thyself,   270
For that which thou hast sworn to do amiss
Is not amiss when it is truly done,
And being not done, where doing tends to ill,
The truth is then most done not doing it:
The better act of purposes mistook
Is to mistake again; though indirect,
Yet indirection thereby grows direct,
And falsehood falsehood cures, as fire cools fire
Within the scorched veins of one new-burn'd.
It is religion that doth make vows kept;   280
But thou hast sworn against religion,
By what thou swear'st against the thing thou swear'st,
And makest an oath the surety for thy truth
Against an oath: the truth thou art unsure
To swear, swears only not to be forsworn;

---

260 *mortal*] deadly, fatal.

271–274 *For that which … doing it*] The meaning of this negative mode of reason-
    ing is that wrong, which you have sworn to do, is not wrong when the
    dictates of truth or rectitude are followed (and the act is not done); (the calls
    of) rectitude are best satisfied, when action which tends to evil is left undone.

276 *indirect*] wrong.

281–285 *But thou hast sworn … not to be forsworn*] Thou hast sworn against the
    dictates of religion by the oath (of alliance with England) which thou art
    taking against thy sworn obligation (to be champion of the church), and
    thou art making an oath (this oath to King John) a certainty or guarantee
    of perjury *(i.e.,* of thy truth against, of thy defiance of, an oath to the
    church): the oath of fidelity to the church (which thou hesitatest to make)
    is an oath that does not admit of perjury.

Else what a mockery should it be to swear!
But thou dost swear only to be forsworn;
And most forsworn, to keep what thou dost swear.
Therefore thy later vows against thy first
Is in thyself rebellion to thyself;   290
And better conquest never canst thou make
Than arm thy constant and thy nobler parts
Against these giddy loose suggestions:
Upon which better part our prayers come in,
If thou vouchsafe them. But if not, then know
The peril of our curses light on thee
So heavy as thou shalt not shake them off,
But in despair die under their black weight.
    AUST. Rebellion, flat rebellion!
    BAST.   Will 't not be?
Will not a calf's-skin stop that mouth of thine?   300
    LEW. Father, to arms!
    BLANCH.   Upon thy wedding-day?
Against the blood that thou hast married?
What, shall our feast be kept with slaughtered men?
Shall braying trumpets and loud churlish drums,
Clamours of hell, be measures to our pomp?
O husband, hear me! ay, alack, how new
Is husband in my mouth! even for that name,
Which till this time my tongue did ne'er pronounce,
Upon my knee I beg, go not to arms
Against mine uncle.
    CONST.   O, upon my knee,   310
Made hard with kneeling, I do pray to thee,
Thou virtuous Dauphin, alter not the doom
Forethought by heaven!
    BLANCH. Now shall I see thy love: what motive may
Be stronger with thee than the name of wife?
    CONST. That which upholdeth him that thee upholds,
His honour: O, thine honour, Lewis, thine honour!

---

293 *suggestions*] temptations.
305 *measures*] slow musical accompaniments, slow dance-tunes.

LEW. I muse your majesty doth seem so cold,
When such profound respects do pull you on.

    PAND. I will denounce a curse upon his head.   320

    K. PHI. Thou shalt not need. England, I will fall from thee.

    CONST. O fair return of banish'd majesty!

    ELI. O foul revolt of French inconstancy!

    K. JOHN. France, thou shalt rue this hour within this hour.

    BAST. Old Time the clock-setter, that bald sexton Time,
Is it as he will? well then, France shall rue.

    BLANCH. The sun's o'ercast with blood: fair day, adieu!
Which is the side that I must go withal?
I am with both: each army hath a hand;
And in their rage, I having hold of both,   330
They whirl asunder and dismember me.
Husband, I cannot pray that thou mayst win;
Uncle, I needs must pray that thou mayst lose;
Father, I may not wish the fortune thine;
Grandam, I will not wish thy wishes thrive:
Whoever wins, on that side shall I lose;
Assured loss before the match be play'd.

    LEW. Lady, with me, with me thy fortune lies.

    BLANCH. There where my fortune lives, there my life dies.

    K. JOHN. Cousin, go draw our puissance together.   340

                             [*Exit Bastard.*
France, I am burn'd up with inflaming wrath;
A rage whose heat hath this condition,
That nothing can allay, nothing but blood,
The blood, and dearest-valued blood, of France.

    K. PHI. Thy rage shall burn thee up, and thou shalt turn
To ashes, ere our blood shall quench that fire:
Look to thyself, thou art in jeopardy.

    K. JOHN. No more than he that threats. To arms let's hie!

                                   [*Exeunt.*

318 *muse*] wonder.
319 *profound respects*] important considerations.
321 *fall from thee*] revolt from thee.

Scene II. *The Same. Plains Near Angiers.*

Alarums, excursions. Enter the BASTARD, *with* AUSTRIA'S *head*

BAST. Now, by my life, this day grows wondrous hot;
Some airy devil hovers in the sky,
And pours down mischief. Austria's head lie there,
While Philip breathes.

Enter KING JOHN, ARTHUR, *and* HUBERT

K. JOHN. Hubert, keep this boy. Philip, make up:
My mother is assailed in our tent,
And ta'en, I fear.
BAST.   My lord, I rescued her;
Her highness is in safety, fear you not:
But on, my liege; for very little pains
Will bring this labour to an happy end.   [*Exeunt.* 10

Scene III. *The Same.*

Alarums, excursions, retreat. Enter KING JOHN, ELINOR, ARTHUR,
the BASTARD, HUBERT, *and* Lords

K. JOHN. [*To Elinor*] So shall it be; your grace shall stay behind
So strongly guarded. [*To Arthur*] Cousin, look not sad:
Thy grandam loves thee; and thy uncle will
As dear be to thee as thy father was.
ARTH. O, this will make my mother die with grief!
K. JOHN. [*To the Bastard*] Cousin, away for England! haste
        before:
And, ere our coming, see thou shake the bags
Of hoarding abbots; imprisoned angels
Set at liberty: the fat ribs of peace

---

2 *airy*] aerial.
5 *Philip*] The Bastard's original name, which King John changed to Richard.
   Philip is the king of France.
   make up] hurry up, make haste.
III, 8 *angels*] gold coins.

Must by the hungry now be fed upon: 10
Use our commission in his utmost force.
    BAST. Bell, book, and candle shall not drive me back,
When gold and silver becks me to come on.
I leave your highness. Grandam, I will pray,
If ever I remember to be holy,
For your fair safety; so, I kiss your hand.
    ELI. Farewell, gentle cousin.
    K. JOHN.   Coz, farewell.
                                          [*Exit Bastard.*
    ELI. Come hither, little kinsman; hark, a word.
    K. JOHN. Come hither, Hubert. O my gentle Hubert,
We owe thee much! within this wall of flesh
There is a soul counts thee her creditor,   20
And with advantage means to pay thy love:
And, my good friend, thy voluntary oath
Lives in this bosom, dearly cherished.
Give me thy hand. I had a thing to say,
But I will fit it with some better time.
By heaven, Hubert, I am almost ashamed
To say what good respect I have of thee.
    HUB. I am much bounden to your majesty.
    K. JOHN. Good friend, thou hast no cause to say so yet,
But thou shalt have; and creep time ne'er so slow,   30
Yet it shall come for me to do thee good.
I had a thing to say, but let it go:
The sun is in the heaven, and the proud day,
Attended with the pleasures of the world,
Is all too wanton and too full of gawds
To give me audience: if the midnight bell
Did, with his iron tongue and brazen mouth,
Sound on into the drowsy ear of night;
If this same were a churchyard where we stand,
And thou possessed with a thousand wrongs;
Or if that surly spirit, melancholy,   40
Had baked thy blood and made it heavy-thick,

---

11 *Bell, book, and candle*] Implements of an ecclesiastical curse or excommuni-
    cation.
21 *advantage*] interest.
35 *gawds*] showy, idle ornaments.

Which else runs tickling up and down the veins,
Making that idiot, laughter, keep men's eyes
And strain their cheeks to idle merriment,
A passion hateful to my purposes;
Or if that thou couldst see me without eyes,
Hear me without thine ears, and make reply
Without a tongue, using conceit alone,
Without eyes, ears and harmful sound of words;
Then, in despite of brooded watchful day,   50
I would into thy bosom pour my thoughts:
But, ah, I will not! yet I love thee well;
And, by my troth, I think thou lovest me well.

  HUB. So well, that what you bid me undertake,
Though that my death were adjunct to my act,
By heaven, I would do it.

  K. JOHN.   Do not I know thou wouldst?
Good Hubert, Hubert, Hubert, throw thine eye
On yon young boy: I'll tell thee what, my friend,
He is a very serpent in my way;
And wheresoe'er this foot of mine doth tread,   60
He lies before me: dost thou understand me?
Thou art his keeper.

  HUB.   And I'll keep him so,
That he shall not offend your majesty.

  K. JOHN.   Death.

  HUB. My lord?

  K. JOHN. A grave.

  HUB.   He shall not live.

  K. JOHN.   Enough.
I could be merry now. Hubert, I love thee;
Well, I'll not say what I intend for thee:
Remember. Madam, fare you well:
I'll send those powers o'er to your majesty.

  ELI. My blessing go with thee!

  K. JOHN.   For England, cousin, go:
Hubert shall be your man, attend on you   70
With all true duty. On toward Calais, ho!   [*Exeunt.*

---

48 *conceit*] thought.

50 *brooded watchful day*] brooding vigilant day. The day is as vigilant, as open-
  eyed, as an animal with a brood (to guard).

SCENE IV. *The Same. The French King's Tent.*

Enter KING PHILIP, LEWIS, PANDULPH, *and* Attendants

K. PHI. So, by a roaring tempest on the flood,
A whole armado of convicted sail
Is scattered and disjoin'd from fellowship.
    PAND. Courage and comfort! all shall yet go well.
    K. PHI. What can go well, when we have run so ill?
Are we not beaten? Is not Angiers lost?
Arthur ta'en prisoner? divers dear friends slain?
And bloody England into England gone,
O'erbearing interruption, spite of France?
    LEW. What he hath won, that hath he fortified: 10
So hot a speed with such advice disposed,
Such temperate order in so fierce a cause,
Doth want example: who hath read or heard
Of any kindred action like to this?
    K. PHI. Well could I bear that England had this praise,
So we could find some pattern of our shame.

Enter CONSTANCE

Look, who comes here! a grave unto a soul;
Holding the eternal spirit, against her will,
In the vile prison of afflicted breath.
I prithee, lady, go away with me.   20
    CONST. Lo, now! now see the issue of your peace.
    K. PHI. Patience, good lady! comfort, gentle Constance!
    CONST. No, I defy all counsel, all redress,
But that which ends all counsel, true redress,

---

2 *armado of convicted sail*] armament or fleet of conquered or beaten sailing
    vessels.
6–7 *Angiers lost? Arthur ta'en prisoner?*] These events were not historically syn-
    chronous. Arthur's capture happened in 1202; the fall of Angiers four years
    later.
9 *O'erbearing interruption*] Putting down attempts to bar the way.
11 *with such advice disposed*] with such judgment regulated.
12 *cause*] action, course of action.
16 *some pattern*] some justifying precedent.

Death, death; O amiable lovely death!
Thou odoriferous stench! sound rottenness!
Arise forth from the couch of lasting night,
Thou hate and terror to prosperity,
And I will kiss thy detestable bones
And put my eyeballs in thy vaulty brows 30
And ring these fingers with thy household worms
And stop this gap of breath with fulsome dust
And be a carrion monster like thyself:
Come, grin on me, and I will think thou smilest,
And buss thee as thy wife. Misery's love,
O, come to me!
    K. PHI.   O fair affliction, peace!
    CONST. No, no, I will not, having breath to cry:
O, that my tongue were in the thunder's mouth!
Then with a passion would I shake the world;
And rouse from sleep that fell anatomy 40
Which cannot hear a lady's feeble voice,
Which scorns a modern invocation.
    PAND. Lady, you utter madness, and not sorrow.
    CONST. Thou art not holy to belie me so;
I am not mad: this hair I tear is mine;
My name is Constance; I was Geffrey's wife;
Young Arthur is my son, and he is lost:
I am not mad: I would to heaven I were!
For then, 't is like I should forget myself:
O, if I could, what grief should I forget! 50
Preach some philosophy to make me mad,
And thou shalt be canonized, cardinal;
For, being not mad but sensible of grief,
My reasonable part produces reason
How I may be deliver'd of these woes,
And teaches me to kill or hang myself:
If I were mad, I should forget my son,
Or madly think a babe of clouts were he:
I am not mad; too well, too well I feel

---

32 *gap of breath*] outlet of breath, mouth.
35 *buss*] kiss.
    Misery's love] Death is courted by misery.
42 *modern*] commonplace.
58 *a babe of clouts*] a rag-doll.

The different plague of each calamity.   60
    K. PHI. Bind up those tresses. O, what love I note
In the fair multitude of those her hairs!
Where but by chance a silver drop hath fallen,
Even to that drop ten thousand wiry friends
Do glue themselves in sociable grief,
Like true, inseparable, faithful loves,
Sticking together in calamity.
    CONST. To England, if you will.
    K. PHI.   Bind up your hairs.
    CONST. Yes, that I will; and wherefore will I do it?
I tore them from their bonds and cried aloud,   70
"O that these hands could so redeem my son,
As they have given these hairs their liberty!"
But now I envy at their liberty,
And will again commit them to their bonds,
Because my poor child is a prisoner.
And, father cardinal, I have heard you say
That we shall see and know our friends in heaven:
If that be true, I shall see my boy again;
For since the birth of Cain, the first male child,
To him that did but yesterday suspire,   80
There was not such a gracious creature born.
But now will canker sorrow eat my bud
And chase the native beauty from his cheek
And he will look as hollow as a ghost,
As dim and meagre as an ague's fit,
And so he'll die; and, rising so again,
When I shall meet him in the court of heaven
I shall not know him: therefore never, never
Must I behold my pretty Arthur more.
    PAND. You hold too heinous a respect of grief.   90

---

64 *friends*] Rowe's emendation of the original reading *fiends*.

68 *To England, if you will*] Constance appears to be answering the appeal addressed to her by King Philip at line 20, *supra:* "I prithee, lady, go away with me."

80 *suspire*] breathe.

82 *canker sorrow*] sorrow like a canker-worm.

90 *You hold ... grief*] You commit heinous sin in paying excessive regard to your grief, in making too much of it.

CONST. He talks to me that never had a son.

K. PHI. You are as fond of grief as of your child.

CONST. Grief fills the room up of my absent child,
Lies in his bed, walks up and down with me,
Puts on his pretty looks, repeats his words,
Remembers me of all his gracious parts,
Stuffs out his vacant garments with his form;
Then have I reason to be fond of grief.
Fare you well: had you such a loss as I,
I could give better comfort than you do.   100
I will not keep this form upon my head,
When there is such disorder in my wit.
O Lord! my boy, my Arthur, my fair son!
My life, my joy, my food, my all the world!
My widow-comfort, and my sorrows' cure!   [*Exit.*

K. PHI. I fear some outrage, and I'll follow her.   [*Exit.*

LEW. There's nothing in this world can make me joy:
Life is as tedious as a twice-told tale
Vexing the dull ear of a drowsy man;
And bitter shame hath spoil'd the sweet world's taste,   110
That it yields nought but shame and bitterness.

PAND. Before the curing of a strong disease,
Even in the instant of repair and health,
The fit is strongest; evils that take leave,
On their departure most of all show evil:
What have you lost by losing of this day?

LEW. All days of glory, joy and happiness.

PAND. If you had won it, certainly you had.
No, no; when Fortune means to men most good,
She looks upon them with a threatening eye.   120
'T is strange to think how much King John hath lost
In this which he accounts so clearly won:
Are not you grieved that Arthur is his prisoner?

LEW. As heartily as he is glad he hath him.

PAND. Your mind is all as youthful as your blood.
Now hear me speak with a prophetic spirit;
For even the breath of what I mean to speak
Shall blow each dust, each straw, each little rub,

---

96 *parts*] qualities.
128 *rub*] technical term for obstruction in the game of bowls.

Out of the path which shall directly lead
Thy foot to England's throne; and therefore mark.   130
John hath seized Arthur; and it cannot be
That, whiles warm life plays in that infant's veins,
The misplaced John should entertain an hour,
One minute, nay, one quiet breath of rest.
A sceptre snatch'd with an unruly hand
Must be as boisterously maintain'd as gain'd;
And he that stands upon a slippery place
Makes nice of no vile hold to stay him up:
That John may stand, then Arthur needs must fall;
So be it, for it cannot be but so.   140
    LEW. But what shall I gain by young Arthur's fall?
    PAND. You, in the right of Lady Blanch your wife,
May then make all the claim that Arthur did.
    LEW. And lose it, life and all, as Arthur did.
    PAND. How green you are and fresh in this old world!
John lays you plots; the times conspire with you;
For he that steeps his safety in true blood
Shall find but bloody safety and untrue.
This act so evilly born shall cool the hearts
Of all his people and freeze up their zeal,   150
That none so small advantage shall step forth
To check his reign, but they will cherish it;
No natural exhalation in the sky,
No scope of nature, no distemper'd day,
No common wind, no customed event,
But they will pluck away his natural cause
And call them meteors, prodigies and signs,
Abortives, presages and tongues of heaven,
Plainly denouncing vengeance upon John.
    LEW. May be he will not touch young Arthur's life,   160
But hold himself safe in his prisonment.
    PAND. O, sir, when he shall hear of your approach,
If that young Arthur be not gone already,

---

138 *Makes nice of*] Scrupulous about, sticks at.
146 *John lays you plots*] John lays plots in your interest.
147 *true blood*] pure, innocent blood.
154 *No scope of nature*] Nothing falling within the ordinary scope of nature.
156 *his natural cause*] its (the event's) natural cause.
158 *Abortives*] Abortions.

Even at that news he dies; and then the hearts
Of all his people shall revolt from him,
And kiss the lips of unacquainted change,
And pick strong matter of revolt and wrath
Out of the bloody fingers' ends of John.
Methinks I see this hurly all on foot:
And, O, what better matter breeds for you   170
Than I have named! The bastard Faulconbridge
Is now in England, ransacking the church,
Offending charity: if but a dozen French
Were there in arms, they would be as a call
To train ten thousand English to their side,
Or as a little snow, tumbled about,
Anon becomes a mountain. O noble Dauphin,
Go with me to the king: 't is wonderful
What may be wrought out of their discontent,
Now that their souls are topful of offence.   180
For England go: I will whet on the king.

    LEW. Strong reasons make strong actions: let us go:
If you say ay, the king will not say no.   [*Exeunt.*

---

166 *unacquainted*] unknown, unwonted.
169 *hurly*] uproar, tumult; a form of hurlyburly.
174–175 *a call To train*] a cry to allure or entice.

ACT IV.

Scene I. *A Room in a Castle.*

Enter Hubert *and* Executioners

Hubert. Heat me these irons hot; and look thou stand
Within the arras: when I strike my foot
Upon the bosom of the ground, rush forth,
And bind the boy which you shall find with me
Fast to the chair: be heedful: hence, and watch.
   First Exec. I hope your warrant will bear out the deed.
   Hub. Uncleanly scruples! fear not you: look to 't.

                                       [Exeunt Executioners.
Young lad, come forth; I have to say with you.

Enter Arthur

   Arth. Good morrow, Hubert.
   Hub.   Good morrow, little prince.
   Arth. As little prince, having so great a title   10
To be more prince, as may be. You are sad.
   Hub. Indeed, I have been merrier.
   Arth.   Mercy on me!
Methinks no body should be sad but I:
Yet, I remember, when I was in France,
Young gentlemen would be as sad as night,
Only for wantonness. By my Christendom,
So I were out of prison and kept sheep,
I should be as merry as the day is long;
And so I would be here, but that I doubt
My uncle practises more harm to me: 20

---

2 *Within the arras*] Behind the tapestry or hangings.
3 *the bosom*] the surface.
7 *Uncleanly scruples*] Hubert is speaking hastily and denounces as "foul" any
    doubt of his commission.
16 *for wantonness*] for freakishness or whimsical affectation. It was at one time a
    fashionable craze among Elizabethan youths to pretend a deep melancholy.
    Christendom] faith as a Christian.
19 *doubt*] fear.
20 *practises*] wickedly contrives.

51

He is afraid of me and I of him:
Is it my fault that I was Geffrey's son?
No, indeed, is 't not; and I would to heaven
I were your son, so you would love me, Hubert.

   HUB. [*Aside*] If I talk to him, with his innocent prate
He will awake my mercy which lies dead:
Therefore I will be sudden and dispatch.

   ARTH. Are you sick, Hubert? you look pale to-day:
In sooth, I would you were a little sick,
That I might sit all night and watch with you: 30
I warrant I love you more than you do me.

   HUB. [*Aside*] His words do take possession of my bosom.
Read here, young Arthur.   [*Showing a paper.*
                  [*Aside*] How now, foolish rheum!
Turning dispiteous torture out of door!
I must be brief, lest resolution drop
Out at mine eyes in tender womanish tears.
Can you not read it? is it not fair writ?

   ARTH. Too fairly, Hubert, for so foul effect:
Must you with hot irons burn out both mine eyes?

   HUB. Young boy, I must.

   ARTH.   And will you?

   HUB.   And I will.   40

   ARTH. Have you the heart? When your head did but ache,
I knit my handkercher about your brows,
The best I had, a princess wrought it me,
And I did never ask it you again;
And with my hand at midnight held your head,
And like the watchful minutes to the hour,
Still and anon cheer'd up the heavy time,
Saying, "What lack you?" and "Where lies your grief?"
Or "What good love may I perform for you?"
Many a poor man's son would have lien still   50
And ne'er have spoke a loving word to you;
But you at your sick service had a prince.
Nay, you may think my love was crafty love,

---

34 *dispiteous*] pitiless.
46 *watchful minutes to the hour*] minutes which keep regular and faithful watch
    while the hour is completing its course.
47 *Still and anon*] Every now and then.
52 *at your sick service*] at your service in your sickness.

And call it cunning: do, an if you will:
If heaven be pleased that you must use me ill,
Why then you must. Will you put out mine eyes?
These eyes that never did nor never shall
So much as frown on you.

    HUB.   I have sworn to do it;
And with hot irons must I burn them out.

    ARTH. Ah, none but in this iron age would do it!   60
The iron of itself, though heat red-hot,
Approaching near these eyes, would drink my tears
And quench his fiery indignation
Even in the matter of mine innocence;
Nay, after that, consume away in rust,
But for containing fire to harm mine eye.
Are you more stubborn-hard than hammer'd iron?
An if an angel should have come to me
And told me Hubert should put out mine eyes,
I would not have believed him,—no tongue but Hubert's.   70

    HUB. Come forth.   [*Stamps.*

Re-enter Executioners, *with a cord, irons, &c.*

Do as I bid you do.

    ARTH. O, save me, Hubert, save me! my eyes are out
Even with the fierce looks of these bloody men.

    HUB. Give me the iron, I say, and bind him here.

    ARTH. Alas, what need you be so boisterous-rough?
I will not struggle, I will stand stone-still.
For heaven sake, Hubert, let me not be bound!
Nay, hear me, Hubert, drive these men away,
And I will sit as quiet as a lamb;   80
I will not stir, nor wince, nor speak a word,
Nor look upon the iron angerly:
Thrust but these men away, and I'll forgive you,
Whatever torment you do put me to.

    HUB. Go, stand within; let me alone with him.

    FIRST EXEC. I am best pleased to be from such a deed.

                            [*Exeunt Executioners.*

    ARTH. Alas, I then have chid away my friend!

---

63 *his*] its.

He hath a stern look, but a gentle heart:
Let him come back, that his compassion may
Give life to yours.

ARTH. Is there no remedy?

HUB.　　　　　　　　　Come, boy, prepare yourself.　　　90

HUB.　　　　　　　　　None, but to lose your eyes.

ARTH. O heaven, that there were but a mote in yours,
A grain, a dust, a gnat, a wandering hair,
Any annoyance in that precious sense!
Then, feeling what small things are boisterous there,
Your vile intent must needs seem horrible.

HUB. Is this your promise? go to, hold your tongue.

ARTH. Hubert, the utterance of a brace of tongues
Must needs want pleading for a pair of eyes:
Let me not hold my tongue, let me not, Hubert;　　　100
Or, Hubert, if you will, cut out my tongue,
So I may keep mine eyes: O, spare mine eyes,
Though to no use but still to look on you!
Lo, by my troth, the instrument is cold
And would not harm me.

HUB.　　　　　　　　　I can heat it, boy.

ARTH. No, in good sooth; the fire is dead with grief,
Being create for comfort, to be used
In undeserved extremes: see else yourself;
There is no malice in this burning coal;
The breath of heaven hath blown his spirit out　　　110
And strew'd repentant ashes on his head.

HUB. But with my breath I can revive it, boy.

ARTH. An if you do, you will but make it blush
And glow with shame of your proceedings, Hubert:
Nay, it perchance will sparkle in your eyes;
And like a dog that is compell'd to fight,
Snatch at his master that doth tarre him on.
All things that you should use to do me wrong
Deny their office: only you do lack
That mercy which fierce fire and iron extends,　　　120

---

99 *want pleading*] lack power of pleading.
107–108 *to be used In undeserved extremes*] at being used in extreme acts of cruelty which are unmerited.
117 *Snatch ... tarre*] Snap ... incite to fight.

Creatures of note for mercy-lacking uses.

HUB. Well, see to live; I will not touch thine eye
For all the treasure that thine uncle owes:
Yet am I sworn and I did purpose, boy,
With this same very iron to burn them out.

ARTH. O, now you look like Hubert! all this while
You were disguised.

HUB.   Peace; no more. Adieu.
Your uncle must not know but you are dead;
I'll fill these dogged spies with false reports:
And, pretty child, sleep doubtless and secure,   130
That Hubert, for the wealth of all the world,
Will not offend thee.

ARTH.   O heaven! I thank you, Hubert.

HUB. Silence; no more: go closely in with me:
Much danger do I undergo for thee.   [_Exeunt._

SCENE II. *King John's Palace.*

Enter KING JOHN, PEMBROKE, SALISBURY, *and other* Lords

K. JOHN. Here once again we sit, once again crown'd,
And look'd upon, I hope, with cheerful eyes.

PEM. This "once again," but that your highness pleased,
Was once superfluous: you were crown'd before,
And that high royalty was ne'er pluck'd off,
The faiths of men ne'er stained with revolt;
Fresh expectation troubled not the land
With any long'd-for change or better state.

SAL. Therefore, to be possess'd with double pomp,
To guard a title that was rich before,   10
To gild refined gold, to paint the lily,

---

121 _Creatures ... uses_] Things famous for their cruel uses.
130 _doubtless and secure_] without fear and in confidence.
132 _offend_] hurt.
133 _closely_] secretly.
4 _once superfluous_] once too often.
10 _guard_] ornament with trimmings, fringe, or facings.

To throw a perfume on the violet,
To smooth the ice, or add another hue
Unto the rainbow, or with taper-light
To seek the beauteous eye of heaven to garnish,
Is wasteful and ridiculous excess.

PEM. But that your royal pleasure must be done,
This act is as an ancient tale new told,
And in the last repeating troublesome,
Being urged at a time unseasonable.   20

SAL. In this the antique and well noted face
Of plain old form is much disfigured;
And, like a shifted wind unto a sail,
It makes the course of thoughts to fetch about,
Startles and frights consideration,
Makes sound opinion sick and truth suspected,
For putting on so new a fashion'd robe.

PEM. When workmen strive to do better than well,
They do confound their skill in covetousness;
And oftentimes excusing of a fault   30
Doth make the fault the worse by the excuse,
As patches set upon a little breach
Discredit more in hiding of the fault
Than did the fault before it was so patch'd.

SAL. To this effect, before you were new crown'd,
We breathed our counsel: but it pleased your highness
To overbear it, and we are all well pleased,
Since all and every part of what we would
Doth make a stand at what your highness will.

K. JOHN. Some reasons of this double coronation   40
I have possess'd you with and think them strong;
And more, more strong, then lesser is my fear,
I shall indue you with: meantime but ask

---

24 *fetch about*] tack about, take a devious course, veer round.

29 *covetousness*] over-eager anxiety to excel others, to win fame.

32 *breach*] rent, tear.

38–39 *Since all ... your highness will*] Since all our desires stop short at, yield to,
    the will of your highness.

42–43 *And more, more strong ... indue you with*] The meaning seems to be: "I shall
    impart to you many more and more powerful reasons for my double corona-
    tion, and then my fear (of your disapproval) will proportionately grow less."

What you would have reform'd that is not well,
And well shall you perceive how willingly
I will both hear and grant you your requests.
   PEM. Then I, as one that am the tongue of these,
To sound the purposes of all their hearts,
Both for myself and them, but, chief of all,
Your safety, for the which myself and them   50
Bend their best studies, heartily request
The enfranchisement of Arthur; whose restraint
Doth move the murmuring lips of discontent
To break into this dangerous argument,—
If what in rest you have in right you hold,
Why then your fears, which as they say, attend
The steps of wrong, should move you to mew up
Your tender kinsman, and to choke his days
With barbarous ignorance, and deny his youth
The rich advantage of good exercise?   60
That the time's enemies may not have this
To grace occasions, let it be our suit
That you have bid us ask his liberty;
Which for our goods we do no further ask
Than whereupon our weal, on you depending,
Counts it your weal he have his liberty.

Enter HUBERT

   K. JOHN. Let it be so: I do commit his youth
To your direction. Hubert, what news with you?
                           [*Taking him apart.*
   PEM. This is the man should do the bloody deed;

---

48 *sound*] express, disclose.

50 *myself and them*] myself and they: a careless repetition of these words from
    the previous line.

55 *If what in rest ... you hold*] If what you have peaceful and secure possession
    of, you hold lawfully.

57 *mew up*] confine: used technically of hawks.

61–62 *That the time's enemies ... To grace occasions*] That agitators against the
    settled order of the age shall not have this cry to improve their opportuni-
    ties of attack, to grace their campaign.

64–66 *Which for our goods ... his liberty*] Which we ask for our advantage, only
    in so far as study of our welfare, which is dependent on you, reckons it to
    be for your welfare and to your benefit that Arthur should have his liberty.

He show'd his warrant to a friend of mine: 70
The image of a wicked heinous fault
Lives in his eye; that close aspect of his
Does show the mood of a much troubled breast;
And I do fearfully believe 't is done,
What we so fear'd he had a charge to do.

SAL. The colour of the king doth come and go
Between his purpose and his conscience,
Like heralds 'twixt two dreadful battles set:
His passion is so ripe, it needs must break.

PEM. And when it breaks, I fear will issue thence   80
The foul corruption of a sweet child's death.

K. JOHN. We cannot hold mortality's strong hand:
Good lords, although my will to give is living,
The suit which you demand is gone and dead:
He tells us Arthur is deceased to-night.

SAL. Indeed we fear'd his sickness was past cure.

PEM. Indeed we heard how near his death he was,
Before the child himself felt he was sick:
This must be answer'd either here or hence.

K. JOHN. Why do you bend such solemn brows on me?   90
Think you I bear the shears of destiny?
Have I commandment on the pulse of life?

SAL. It is apparent foul-play; and 't is shame
That greatness should so grossly offer it:
So thrive it in your game! and so, farewell.

PEM. Stay yet, Lord Salisbury; I'll go with thee,
And find the inheritance of this poor child,
His little kingdom of a forced grave.
That blood which owed the breadth of all this isle,
Three foot of it doth hold: bad world the while!   100
This must not be thus borne: this will break out
To all our sorrows, and ere long I doubt.   [*Exeunt Lords.*

---

72 *close aspect*] look of secrecy.
77 *his purpose*] his wicked purpose of murdering Arthur.
78 *battles*] armies in battle array.
79 *His passion ... break*] The image is that of a boil or tumour.
93 *apparent*] manifest.
95 *So thrive it in your game!*] Shamefully may your greatness thrive in the game
   you are playing!
102 *doubt*] fear.

K. JOHN. They burn in indignation. I repent:
There is no sure foundation set on blood,
No certain life achieved by others' death.

Enter a Messenger

A fearful eye thou hast: where is that blood
That I have seen inhabit in those cheeks?
So foul a sky clears not without a storm:
Pour down thy weather: how goes all in France?
  MESS. From France to England. Never such a power 110
For any foreign preparation
Was levied in the body of a land.
The copy of your speed is learn'd by them;
For when you should be told they do prepare,
The tidings comes that they are all arrived.
  K. JOHN. O, where hath our intelligence been drunk?
Where hath it slept? Where is my mother's care,
That such an army could be drawn in France,
And she not hear of it?
  MESS.   My liege, her ear
Is stopp'd with dust; the first of April died 120
Your noble mother: and, as I hear, my lord,
The Lady Constance in a frenzy died
Three days before: but this from rumour's tongue
I idly heard; if true or false I know not.
  K. JOHN. Withhold thy speed, dreadful occasion!
O, make a league with me, till I have pleased
My discontented peers! What! mother dead!
How wildly then walks my estate in France!
Under whose conduct came those powers of France

---

106 *fearful*] full of fear, frightened.
110 *From France to England*] "All goes from France to invade England;" a quib-
  bling reply to the question "How goes all in France?"
118 *drawn*] levied.
120 *the first of April*] This is the precise date of Queen Elinor's death, in the
  year 1204.
122 *The Lady Constance ... died*] Constance predeceased Queen Elinor, in
  1201, by three years, not, as in the text, by three days.
128 *How wildly ... my estate*] How unsteadily goes, how tottering is, the state
  of my affairs.

That thou for truth givest out are landed here?   130
    MESS. Under the Dauphin.
    K. JOHN.   Thou hast made me giddy
With these ill tidings.

Enter the BASTARD *and* PETER *of Pomfret*

                        Now, what says the world
To your proceedings? do not seek to stuff
My head with more ill news, for it is full.
    BAST. But if you be afeard to hear the worst,
Then let the worst unheard fall on your head.
    K. JOHN. Bear with me, cousin; for I was amazed
Under the tide: but now I breathe again
Aloft the flood, and can give audience
To any tongue, speak it of what it will.   140
    BAST. How I have sped among the clergy-men,
The sums I have collected shall express.
But as I travell'd hither through the land,
I find the people strangely fantasied;
Possess'd with rumours, full of idle dreams,
Not knowing what they fear, but full of fear:
And here's a prophet, that I brought with me
From forth the streets of Pomfret, whom I found
With many hundreds treading on his heels;
To whom he sung, in rude harsh-sounding rhymes,   150
That, ere the next Ascension-day at noon,
Your highness should deliver up your crown.
    K. JOHN. Thou idle dreamer, wherefore didst thou so?
    PETER. Foreknowing that the truth will fall out so.
    K. JOHN. Hubert, away with him; imprison him;
And on that day at noon, whereon he says
I shall yield up my crown, let him be hang'd.
Deliver him to safety; and return,

---

138 *Under the tide*] King John compares himself to a swimmer, first, bewildered
    and overwhelmed by the tide (of bad news) and, then, mastering the rush
    of water.
144 *strangely fantasied*] subject to strange fancies.
158 *to safety*] to safe-keeping, safe-custody.

For I must use thee.   [*Exit* HUBERT *with* PETER.
                    O my gentle cousin,
Hear'st thou the news abroad, who are arrived?   160
    BAST. The French, my lord; men's mouths are full of it:
Besides, I met Lord Bigot and Lord Salisbury,
With eyes as red as new-enkindled fire,
And others more, going to seek the grave
Of Arthur, whom they say is kill'd to-night
On your suggestion.
    K. JOHN.   Gentle kinsman, go,
And thrust thyself into their companies:
I have a way to win their loves again;
Bring them before me.
    BAST.   I will seek them out.
    K. JOHN. Nay, but make haste; the better foot before.   170
O, let me have no subject enemies,
When adverse foreigners affright my towns
With dreadful pomp of stout invasion!
Be Mercury, set feathers to thy heels,
And fly like thought from them to me again.
    BAST. The spirit of the time shall teach me speed.   [*Exit.*
    K. JOHN. Spoke like a sprightful noble gentleman.
Go after him; for he perhaps shall need
Some messenger betwixt me and the peers;
And be thou he.
    MESS.   With all my heart, my liege.   [*Exit.* 180
    K. JOHN. My mother dead!

Re-enter HUBERT

    HUB. My lord, they say five moons were seen to-night;
Four fixed, and the fifth did whirl about
The other four in wondrous motion.
    K. JOHN. Five moons!
    HUB.   Old men and beldams in the streets
Do prophesy upon it dangerously:

---

163 *as red*] *sc.* with anger.
171 *subject*] *Subject* must be allotted a plural significance, like "people."

Young Arthur's death is common in their mouths:
And when they talk of him, they shake their heads
And whisper one another in the ear;
And he that speaks doth gripe the hearer's wrist,   190
Whilst he that hears makes fearful action,
With wrinkled brows, with nods, with rolling eyes.
I saw a smith stand with his hammer, thus,
The whilst his iron did on the anvil cool,
With open mouth swallowing a tailor's news;
Who, with his shears and measure in his hand,
Standing on slippers, which his nimble haste
Had falsely thrust upon contrary feet,
Told of a many thousand warlike French
That were embattailed and rank'd in Kent: 200
Another lean unwash'd artificer
Cuts off his tale and talks of Arthur's death.
    K. JOHN. Why seek'st thou to possess me with these fears?
Why urgest thou so oft young Arthur's death?
Thy hand hath murder'd him: I had a mighty cause
To wish him dead, but thou hadst none to kill him.
    HUB. No had, my lord! why, did you not provoke me?
    K. JOHN. It is the curse of kings to be attended
By slaves that take their humours for a warrant
To break within the bloody house of life,   210
And on the winking of authority
To understand a law, to know the meaning
Of dangerous majesty, when perchance it frowns
More upon humour than advised respect.
    HUB. Here is your hand and seal for what I did.
    K. JOHN. O, when the last account 'twixt heaven and earth
Is to be made, then shall this hand and seal
Witness against us to damnation!
How oft the sight of means to do ill deeds
Make deeds ill done! Hadst not thou been by,   220
A fellow by the hand of nature mark'd,

---

198 *contrary feet*] the left foot into the right slipper, and *vice versa*.
200 *embattailed*] drawn up in order of battle.
207 *provoke*] incite.
214 *More … respect*] From mere whim or caprice rather than from deliberate
    judgment.

Quoted and sign'd to do a deed of shame,
This murder had not come into my mind:
But taking note of thy abhorr'd aspect,
Finding thee fit for bloody villany,
Apt, liable to be employ'd in danger,
I faintly broke with thee of Arthur's death;
And thou, to be endeared to a king,
Made it no conscience to destroy a prince.

   HUB. My lord,—   230

   K. JOHN. Hadst thou but shook thy head or made a pause
When I spake darkly what I purposed,
Or turn'd an eye of doubt upon my face,
As bid me tell my tale in express words,
Deep shame had struck me dumb, made me break off,
And those thy fears might have wrought fears in me:
But thou didst understand me by my signs
And didst in signs again parley with sin;
Yea, without stop, didst let thy heart consent,
And consequently thy rude hand to act   240
The deed, which both our tongues held vile to name.
Out of my sight, and never see me more!
My nobles leave me; and my state is braved,
Even at my gates, with ranks of foreign powers:
Nay, in the body of this fleshly land,
This kingdom, this confine of blood and breath,
Hostility and civil tumult reigns
Between my conscience and my cousin's death.

   HUB. Arm you against your other enemies,
I'll make a peace between your soul and you.   250
Young Arthur is alive: this hand of mine
Is yet a maiden and an innocent hand,
Not painted with the crimson spots of blood.
Within this bosom never enter'd yet
The dreadful motion of a murderous thought;
And you have slander'd nature in my form,
Which, howsoever rude exteriorly,

---

222 *Quoted*] The word is often used of books with annotations in the margin
    confirmatory of the text. Here the sense is "fully indicated" or "certified."
226 *liable ... danger*] disposed for employment in designs of danger.
246 *this confine of blood and breath*] my corporeal frame.
255 *motion*] suggestion, prompting.

Is yet the cover of a fairer mind
Than to be butcher of an innocent child.

    K. JOHN. Doth Arthur live? O, haste thee to the peers,   260
Throw this report on their incensed rage,
And make them tame to their obedience!
Forgive the comment that my passion made
Upon thy feature; for my rage was blind,
And foul imaginary eyes of blood
Presented thee more hideous than thou art.
O, answer not, but to my closet bring
The angry lords with all expedient haste.
I conjure thee but slowly; run more fast.   [*Exeunt.*

SCENE III. *Before the Castle.*

Enter ARTHUR, *on the walls*

    ARTH. The wall is high, and yet will I leap down:
Good ground, be pitiful and hurt me not!
There's few or none do know me: if they did,
This ship-boy's semblance hath disguised me quite.
I am afraid; and yet I'll venture it.
If I get down, and do not break my limbs,
I'll find a thousand shifts to get away:
As good to die and go, as die and stay.   [*Leaps down.*
O me! my uncle's spirit is in these stones:
Heaven take my soul, and England keep my bones!   10
                            [*Dies.*

Enter PEMBROKE, SALISBURY, *and* BIGOT

    SAL. Lords, I will meet him at Saint Edmundsbury:
It is our safety, and we must embrace
This gentle offer of the perilous time.
    PEM. Who brought that letter from the cardinal?
    SAL. The Count Melun, a noble lord of France;

---

4 *semblance*] disguise.
11 *him*] *i.e.,* the Dauphin.

Whose private with me of the Dauphin's love
Is much more general than these lines import.
  Big. To-morrow morning let us meet him then.
  Sal. Or rather then set forward; for 't will be
Two long days' journey, lords, or ere we meet.   20

Enter the Bastard

  Bast. Once more to-day well met, distemper'd lords!
The king by me requests your presence straight.
  Sal. The king hath dispossess'd himself of us:
We will not line his thin bestained cloak
With our pure honours, nor attend the foot
That leaves the print of blood where'er it walks.
Return and tell him so: we know the worst.
  Bast. Whate'er you think, good words, I think, were best.
  Sal. Our griefs, and not our manners, reason now.
  Bast. But there is little reason in your grief;   30
Therefore 't were reason you had manners now.
  Pem. Sir, sir, impatience hath his privilege.
  Bast. 'T is true, to hurt his master, no man else.
  Sal. This is the prison. What is he lies here?

                              [Seeing Arthur.

  Pem. O death, made proud with pure and princely beauty!
The earth hath not a hole to hide this deed.
  Sal. Murder, as hating what himself hath done,
Doth lay it open to urge on revenge.
  Big. Or, when doom'd this beauty to a grave,
Found it too precious-princely for a grave.   40
  Sal. Sir Richard, what think you? have you beheld,
Or have you read or heard? or could you think?
Or do you almost think, although you see,
That you do see? could thought, without this object,
Form such another? This is the very top,
The height, the crest, or crest unto the crest,
Of murder's arms: this is the bloodiest shame,

---

16 *Whose private with me*] "Private" must mean elliptically "private talk" or
    "intimation."
17 *general*] ample.
21 *distemper'd*] ruffled, out of temper.
29 *reason*] talk, discourse.

The wildest savagery, the vilest stroke,
That ever wall-eyed wrath or staring rage
Presented to the tears of soft remorse. 50

PEM. All murders past do stand excused in this:
And this, so sole and so unmatchable,
Shall give a holiness, a purity,
To the yet unbegotten sin of times;
And prove a deadly bloodshed but a jest,
Exampled by this heinous spectacle.

BAST. It is a damned and a bloody work;
The graceless action of a heavy hand,
If that it be the work of any hand.

SAL. If that it be the work of any hand! 60
We had a kind of light what would ensue:
It is the shameful work of Hubert's hand;
The practice and the purpose of the king:
From whose obedience I forbid my soul,
Kneeling before this ruin of sweet life,
And breathing to his breathless excellence
The incense of a vow, a holy vow,
Never to taste the pleasures of the world,
Never to be infected with delight,
Nor conversant with ease and idleness, 70
Till I have set a glory to this hand,
By giving it the worship of revenge.

PEM. ⎫
     ⎬ Our souls religiously confirm thy words.
BIG. ⎭

Enter HUBERT

HUB. Lords, I am hot with haste in seeking you:
Arthur doth live; the king hath sent for you.

SAL. O, he is bold and blushes not at death.
Avaunt, thou hateful villain, get thee gone!

HUB. I am no villain.

SAL.   Must I rob the law?

                       [*Drawing his sword.*

---

49 *wall-eyed*] glaring-eyed.

50 *remorse*] pity.

54 *sin of times*] sin of future times.

72 *the worship of revenge*] the honour and dignity due to the performance of an
    act of vengeance.

BAST. Your sword is bright, sir; put it up again.

SAL. Not till I sheathe it in a murderer's skin.   80

HUB. Stand back, Lord Salisbury, stand back, I say;
By heaven, I think my sword's as sharp as yours:
I would not have you, lord, forget yourself,
Nor tempt the danger of my true defence;
Lest I, by marking of your rage, forget
Your worth, your greatness and nobility.

BIG. Out, dunghill! darest thou brave a nobleman?

HUB. Not for my life: but yet I dare defend
My innocent life against an emperor.

SAL. Thou art a murderer.

HUB.   Do not prove me so;   90
Yet I am none: whose tongue soe'er speaks false,
Not truly speaks; who speaks not truly, lies.

PEM. Cut him to pieces.

BAST.   Keep the peace, I say.

SAL. Stand by, or I shall gall you, Faulconbridge.

BAST. Thou wert better gall the devil, Salisbury:
If thou but frown on me, or stir thy foot,
Or teach thy hasty spleen to do me shame,
I'll strike thee dead. Put up thy sword betime;
Or I'll so maul you and your toasting-iron,
That you shall think the devil is come from hell.   100

BIG. What wilt thou do, renowned Faulconbridge?
Second a villain and a murderer?

HUB. Lord Bigot, I am none.

BIG.   Who kill'd this prince?

HUB. 'T is not an hour since I left him well:
I honour'd him, I loved him, and will weep
My date of life out for his sweet life's loss.

SAL. Trust not those cunning waters of his eyes,
For villany is not without such rheum;
And he, long traded in it, makes it seem

---

84 *the danger of my true defence*] the danger of encountering me when making defence of my honesty.

87 *Out, dunghill*] a common term of opprobrium.

90–91 *Do not ... am none*] Do not make me a murderer by forcing me to kill you. Hitherto, as yet, I am no murderer.

94 *gall*] hurt, torment.

106 *date*] term.

109 *traded*] practised.

Like rivers of remorse and innocency.   110
Away with me, all you whose souls abhor
The uncleanly savours of a slaughter-house;
For I am stifled with this smell of sin.

   BIG. Away toward Bury, to the Dauphin there!

   PEM. There tell the king he may inquire us out.

                              [Exeunt Lords.

   BAST. Here's a good world! Knew you of this fair work?
Beyond the infinite and boundless reach
Of mercy, if thou didst this deed of death,
Art thou damn'd, Hubert.

   HUB.   Do but hear me, sir.

   BAST. Ha! I'll tell thee what;   120
Thou 'rt damn'd as black—nay, nothing is so black;
Thou art more deep damn'd than Prince Lucifer:
There is not yet so ugly a fiend of hell
As thou shalt be, if thou didst kill this child.

   HUB. Upon my soul—

   BAST.   If thou didst but consent
To this most cruel act, do but despair;
And if thou want'st a cord, the smallest thread
That ever spider twisted from her womb
Will serve to strangle thee; a rush will be a beam
To hang thee on; or wouldst thou drown thyself,   130
Put but a little water in a spoon,
And it shall be as all the ocean,
Enough to stifle such a villain up.
I do suspect thee very grievously.

   HUB. If I in act, consent, or sin of thought,
Be guilty of the stealing that sweet breath
Which was embounded in this beauteous clay,
Let hell want pains enough to torture me.
I left him well.

   BAST.   Go, bear him in thine arms.
I am amazed, methinks, and lose my way   140
Among the thorns and dangers of this world.

---

110 *remorse*] pity.

121 *damn'd as black*] A possible reminiscence of the blackened faces of those
    who played damned souls in the old miracle plays.

133 *stifle … up*] "up" gives the verb the intensive force of "smother."

137 *embounded*] confined.

How easy dost thou take all England up!
From forth this morsel of dead royalty,
The life, the right and truth of all this realm
Is fled to heaven; and England now is left
To tug and scamble and to part by the teeth
The unowed interest of proud-swelling state.
Now for the bare-pick'd bone of majesty
Doth dogged war bristle his angry crest
And snarleth in the gentle eyes of peace: 150
Now powers from home and discontents at home
Meet in one line; and vast confusion waits,
As doth a raven on a sick-fallen beast,
The imminent decay of wrested pomp.
Now happy he whose cloak and cincture can
Hold out this tempest. Bear away that child
And follow me with speed: I'll to the king:
A thousand businesses are brief in hand,
And heaven itself doth frown upon the land.   [*Exeunt.*

---

146 *scamble*] scramble, scuffle.
147 *unowed*] unowned, not in anybody's legal ownership.
152 *vast*] waste, wasting.
154 *wrested pomp*] greatness riotously wrested from its rightful owner.
155 *cincture*] girdle, belt.
158 *are brief in hand*] press for urgent despatch.

ACT V.

SCENE I. *King John's Palace.*

Enter KING JOHN, PANDULPH, *and* Attendants

KING JOHN. Thus have I yielded up into your hand
The circle of my glory. [*Giving the crown.*
    PAND.   Take again
From this my hand, as holding of the pope
Your sovereign greatness and authority.
    K. JOHN. Now keep your holy word: go meet the French,
And from his holiness use all your power
To stop their marches 'fore we are inflamed.
Our discontented counties do revolt;
Our people quarrel with obedience,
Swearing allegiance and the love of soul   10
To stranger blood, to foreign royalty.
This inundation of mistempered humour
Rests by you only to be qualified:
Then pause not; for the present time's so sick,
That present medicine must be minister'd,
Or overthrow incurable ensues.
    PAND. It was my breath that blew this tempest up,
Upon your stubborn usage of the pope;
But since you are a gentle convertite,
My tongue shall hush again this storm of war,   20
And make fair weather in your blustering land.
On this Ascension-day, remember well,
Upon your oath of service to the pope,
Go I to make the French lay down their arms.   [*Exit.*
    K. JOHN. Is this Ascension-day? Did not the prophet
Say that before Ascension-day at noon
My crown I should give off? Even so I have:

---

2 *The circle*] The crown encircling the head.

7 *inflamed*] in flames, in conflagration.

8 *counties*] counts, noblemen in contract with people in the next line; not
    "shires."

10 *love of soul*] soul-felt love.

12 *mistempered*] disordered.

19 *convertite*] convert; especially a reclaimed apostate.

I did suppose it should be on constraint;
But, heaven be thank'd, it is but voluntary.

Enter the BASTARD

BAST. All Kent hath yielded; nothing there holds out   30
But Dover Castle: London hath received,
Like a kind host, the Dauphin and his powers:
Your nobles will not hear you, but are gone
To offer service to your enemy,
And wild amazement hurries up and down
The little number of your doubtful friends.
    K. JOHN. Would not my lords return to me again,
After they heard young Arthur was alive?
    BAST. They found him dead and cast into the streets,
An empty casket, where the jewel of life   40
By some damn'd hand was robb'd and ta'en away.
    K. JOHN. That villain Hubert told me he did live.
    BAST. So, on my soul, he did, for aught he knew.
But wherefore do you droop? why look you sad?
Be great in act, as you have been in thought;
Let not the world see fear and sad distrust
Govern the motion of a kingly eye:
Be stirring as the time; be fire with fire;
Threaten the threatener, and outface the brow
Of bragging horror: so shall inferior eyes,   50
That borrow their behaviours from the great,
Grow great by your example and put on
The dauntless spirit of resolution.
Away, and glister like the god of war,
When he intendeth to become the field:
Show boldness and aspiring confidence.
What, shall they seek the lion in his den,
And fright him there? and make him tremble there?
O, let it not be said: forage, and run
To meet displeasure farther from the doors,   60

_____

35 *amazement*] panic, bewilderment.
55 *to become the field*] to fit or adorn the field, to join the fight with befitting
    glory.
59 *forage*] range abroad in search of prey.
60 *displeasure*] disaster, annoyance.

And grapple with him ere he come so nigh.

K. JOHN. The legate of the pope hath been with me,
And I have made a happy peace with him;
And he hath promised to dismiss the powers
Led by the Dauphin.

BAST.   O inglorious league!
Shall we, upon the footing of our land,
Send fair-play orders and make compromise,
Insinuation, parley and base truce
To arms invasive? shall a beardless boy,
A cocker'd silken wanton, brave our fields,   70
And flesh his spirit in a warlike soil,
Mocking the air with colours idly spread,
And find no check? Let us, my liege, to arms:
Perchance the cardinal cannot make your peace;
Or if he do, let it at least be said
They saw we had a purpose of defence.

K. JOHN. Have thou the ordering of this present time.

BAST. Away, then, with good courage! yet, I know,
Our party may well meet a prouder foe.   [*Exeunt.*

SCENE II. *The Dauphin's Camp at St Edmundsbury.*

Enter, in arms, LEWIS, SALISBURY, MELUN, PEMBROKE,
BIGOT, *and* Soldiers

LEW. My Lord Melun, let this be copied out,
And keep it safe for our remembrance:
Return the precedent to these lords again;

---

66 *upon the footing of our land*] with our foot on our native land.

67 *fair-play orders*] stipulations of courteous conduct.

68 *Insinuation*] The act of ingratiating oneself, of making up to another.

69 *arms invasive*] invading forces.

70 *A cocker'd silken wanton*] A pampered daintily-arrayed effeminate.

71 *flesh his spirit in a warlike soil*] air his courage in a country of warriors.

78–79 *Away, then, ... prouder foe*] On, then, with good hope. In spite of all omens I know that our side may well be able to cope with a stouter and more confident enemy.

1 *this*] The first draft of the treaty with the English lords, which in line 3 is called "the precedent" (*i.e.*, the original document).

That, having our fair order written down,
Both they and we, perusing o'er these notes,
May know wherefore we took the sacrament
And keep our faiths firm and inviolable.
   SAL. Upon our sides it never shall be broken.
And, noble Dauphin, albeit we swear
A voluntary zeal and an unurged faith   10
To your proceedings; yet believe me, prince,
I am not glad that such a sore of time
Should seek a plaster by contemn'd revolt,
And heal the inveterate canker of one wound
By making many. O, it grieves my soul,
That I must draw this metal from my side
To be a widow-maker! O, and there
Where honourable rescue and defence
Cries out upon the name of Salisbury!
But such is the infection of the time,   20
That, for the health and physic of our right,
We cannot deal but with the very hand
Of stern injustice and confused wrong.
And is't not pity, O my grieved friends,
That we, the sons and children of this isle,
Were born to see so sad an hour as this;
Wherein we step after a stranger, march
Upon her gentle bosom, and fill up
Her enemies' ranks,—I must withdraw and weep
Upon the spot of this enforced cause,—   30
To grace the gentry of a land remote,
And follow unacquainted colours here?
What, here? O nation, that thou couldst remove!
That Neptune's arms, who clippeth thee about,
Would bear thee from the knowledge of thyself,
And grapple thee unto a pagan shore;
Where these two Christian armies might combine

---

4 *our fair order*] our justly-arranged stipulation.
16 *metal*] sword (of iron).
19 *Cries out upon*] Exclaims against.
27 *a stranger*] a foreigner.
30 *Upon ... cause*] Over the disgrace of this compulsory course (of action).
34 *clippeth*] embraceth.

The blood of malice in a vein of league,
And not to spend it so unneighbourly!

LEW. A noble temper dost thou show in this; 40
And great affections wrestling in thy bosom
Doth make an earthquake of nobility.
O, what a noble combat hast thou fought
Between compulsion and a brave respect!
Let me wipe off this honourable dew,
That silverly doth progress on thy cheeks:
My heart hath melted at a lady's tears,
Being an ordinary inundation;
But this effusion of such manly drops,
This shower, blown up by tempest of the soul, 50
Startles mine eyes, and makes me more amazed
Than had I seen the vaulty top of heaven
Figured quite o'er with burning meteors.
Lift up thy brow, renowned Salisbury,
And with a great heart heave away this storm:
Commend these waters to those baby eyes
That never saw the giant world enraged;
Nor met with fortune other than at feasts,
Full of warm blood, of mirth, of gossiping.
Come, come; for thou shalt thrust thy hand as deep 60
Into the purse of rich prosperity
As Lewis himself: so, nobles, shall you all,
That knit your sinews to the strength of mine.
And even there, methinks, an angel spake:

---

38 *in a vein of league*] into a vein of friendship.
39 *to spend*] "to" is grammatically superfluous.
44 *a brave respect*] considerations of honour and manliness.
46 *doth progress*] doth (make its) progress.
52 *vaulty top*] vaulted, vault-like roof.
59 *gossiping*] merry, easy talk.
64 *even there ... an angel spake*] A colloquialism expressive here of slyly ironical
corroboration. Possibly a quibble is intended on the alleged mercenary
motives of the speaker's English allies. The arrogant Dauphin has already
spoken of "the *purse* of rich prosperity," and addressed Salisbury and his
friends as "nobles" (the name of a familiar gold coin). "Angel," which is
the name of another gold coin, may carry on the mercenary insinuation.

Enter PANDULPH

Look, where the holy legate comes apace,
To give us warrant from the hand of heaven,
And on our actions set the name of right
With holy breath.
    PAND.   Hail, noble prince of France!
The next is this, King John hath reconciled
Himself to Rome; his spirit is come in,   70
That so stood out against the holy church,
The great metropolis and see of Rome:
Therefore thy threatening colours now wind up;
And tame the savage spirit of wild war,
That, like a lion foster'd up at hand,
It may lie gently at the foot of peace,
And be no further harmful than in show.
    LEW. Your grace shall pardon me, I will not back:
I am too high-born to be propertied,
To be a secondary at control,   80
Or useful serving-man and instrument
To any sovereign state throughout the world.
Your breath first kindled the dead coal of wars
Between this chastised kingdom and myself,
And brought in matter that should feed this fire;
And now 't is far too huge to be blown out
With that same weak wind which enkindled it.
You taught me how to know the face of right,
Acquainted me with interest to this land,
Yea, thrust this enterprise into my heart;   90
And come ye now to tell me John hath made
His peace with Rome? What is that peace to me?
I, by the honour of my marriage-bed,
After young Arthur, claim this land for mine;
And, now it is half-conquer'd, must I back
Because that John hath made his peace with Rome?

---

75 *foster'd up at hand*] brought up by hand, reared by human care.
79 *to be propertied*] to be treated like a contemptible theatrical property.
80 *a secondary at control*] a subordinate under control.
89 *interest*] the claim I possess.

Am I Rome's slave? What penny hath Rome borne,
What men provided, what munition sent,
To underprop this action? Is 't not I
That undergo this charge? who else but I,   100
And such as to my claim are liable,
Sweat in this business and maintain this war?
Have I not heard these islanders shout out
"Vive le roi!" as I have bank'd their towns?
Have I not here the best cards for the game,
To win this easy match play'd for a crown?
And shall I now give o'er the yielded set?
No, no, on my soul, it never shall be said.

    PAND. You look but on the outside of this work.

    LEW. Outside or inside, I will not return   110
Till my attempt so much be glorified
As to my ample hope was promised
Before I drew this gallant head of war,
And cull'd these fiery spirits from the world,
To outlook conquest and to win renown
Even in the jaws of danger and of death.

                                  [Trumpet sounds.

What lusty trumpet thus doth summon us?

Enter the BASTARD, *attended*

    BAST. According to the fair-play of the world,
Let me have audience; I am sent to speak:
My holy lord of Milan, from the king   120
I come, to learn how you have dealt for him;
And, as you answer, I do know the scope
And warrant limited unto my tongue.

---

104 *bank'd their towns*] passed along the river-banks about their towns.
    "Coasted" is similarly used of vessels at sea.

107 *set*] bout (of a game).

113 *drew this gallant head of war*] levied this gallant fighting force.

115 *To outlook conquest*] To conquer by facing down, intimidating, over-
    aweing (resistance).

118 *the fair-play of the world*] the principles of fair-play recognized by the world.

121 *dealt*] negotiated, acted.

123 *limited*] set as limit, appointed.

PAND. The Dauphin is too wilful-opposite,
And will not temporize with my entreaties;
He flatly says he'll not lay down his arms.
    BAST. By all the blood that ever fury breathed,
The youth says well. Now hear our English king;
For thus his royalty doth speak in me.
He is prepared, and reason too he should: 130
This apish and unmannerly approach,
This harness'd masque and unadvised revel,
This unhair'd sauciness and boyish troops,
The king doth smile at; and is well prepared
To whip this dwarfish war, these pigmy arms,
From out the circle of his territories.
That hand which had the strength, even at your door,
To cudgel you and make you take the hatch,
To dive like buckets in concealed wells,
To crouch in litter of your stable planks,   140
To lie like pawns lock'd up in chests and trunks,
To hug with swine, to seek sweet safety out
In vaults and prisons, and to thrill and shake
Even at the crying of your nation's crow,
Thinking his voice an armed Englishman;
Shall that victorious hand be feebled here,
That in your chambers gave you chastisement?
No: know the gallant monarch is in arms
And like an eagle o'er his aery towers,
To souse annoyance that comes near his nest.   150
And you degenerate, you ingrate revolts,
You bloody Neroes, ripping up the womb

---

124 *wilful-opposite*] wrongheaded.
132 *harness'd masque*] masque in armour.
    unadvised] rash, irresponsible.
138 *take the hatch*] take your departure by leaping the halfdoor, hurry off, take
    a hurried leap.
140 *in litter ... planks*] amid the litter of your stable-floors.
141 *pawns*] pledges in a pawnshop.
144 *your nation's crow*] the crowing cock is the French national bird.
146 *feebled*] enfeebled.
149 *o'er his aery towers*] soars or towers over the brood in his nest.
150 *souse*] pounce on.
151 *revolts*] men in revolt, deserters.

Of your dear mother England, blush for shame;
For your own ladies and pale-visaged maids
Like Amazons come tripping after drums,
Their thimbles into armed gauntlets change,
Their needles to lances, and their gentle hearts
To fierce and bloody inclination.

LEW. There end thy brave, and turn thy face in peace;
We grant thou canst outscold us: fare thee well;   160
We hold our time too precious to be spent
With such a brabbler.

PAND.   Give me leave to speak.

BAST. No, I will speak.

LEW.   We will attend to neither.
Strike up the drums; and let the tongue of war
Plead for our interest and our being here.

BAST. Indeed, your drums, being beaten, will cry out;
And so shall you, being beaten: do but start
An echo with the clamour of thy drum,
And even at hand a drum is ready braced
That shall reverberate all as loud as thine;   170
Sound but another, and another shall
As loud as thine rattle the welkin's ear
And mock the deep-mouth'd thunder: for at hand,
Not trusting to this halting legate here,
Whom he hath used rather for sport than need,
Is warlike John; and in his forehead sits
A bare-ribb'd death, whose office is this day
To feast upon whole thousands of the French.

LEW. Strike up our drums, to find this danger out.

BAST. And thou shalt find it, Dauphin, do not doubt.   180

                                        [*Exeunt.*

---

156 *armed*] plated with steel.
159 *brave*] bravado, boasting.
162 *brabbler*] brawler.
165 *interest*] claim.
172 *rattle the welkin's ear*] rattle in the ear of heaven.
173 *deep-mouth'd*] deep-voiced.
177 *A bare-ribb'd death*] A skeleton.

SCENE III. *The Field of Battle.*

Alarums. Enter KING JOHN *and* HUBERT

K. JOHN. How goes the day with us? O, tell me, Hubert.
HUB. Badly, I fear. How fares your majesty?
K. JOHN. This fever, that hath troubled me so long,
Lies heavy on me; O, my heart is sick!

Enter a Messenger

MESS. My lord, your valiant kinsman, Faulconbridge,
Desires your majesty to leave the field
And send him word by me which way you go.
K. JOHN. Tell him, toward Swinstead, to the abbey there.
MESS. Be of good comfort; for the great supply
That was expected by the Dauphin here,   10
Are wreck'd three nights ago on Goodwin Sands.
This news was brought to Richard but even now:
The French fight coldly, and retire themselves.
K. JOHN. Ay me! this tyrant fever burns me up,
And will not let me welcome this good news.
Set on towards Swinstead: to my litter straight;
Weakness possesseth me, and I am faint.   [*Exeunt.*

SCENE IV. *Another Part of the Field.*

Enter SALISBURY, PEMBROKE, *and* BIGOT

SAL. I did not think the king so stored with friends.
PEM. Up once again; put spirit in the French:
If they miscarry, we miscarry too.
SAL. That misbegotten devil, Faulconbridge,
In spite of spite, alone upholds the day.
PEM. They say King John sore sick hath left the field.

---

9 *supply*] reinforcement; a noun of multitude.
12 *Richard*] the Bastard.
13 *retire themselves*] withdraw themselves, retreat.
16 *Swinstead*] Swineshead, near Spalding in Lincolnshire.
IV, 5 *In spite of spite*] Despite all disaster.

Enter MELUN, *wounded*

MEL. Lead me to the revolts of England here.
SAL. When we were happy we had other names.
PEM. It is the Count Melun.
SAL.   Wounded to death.
MEL. Fly, noble English, you are bought and sold;   10
Unthread the rude eye of rebellion
And welcome home again discarded faith.
Seek out King John and fall before his feet;
For if the French be lords of this loud day,
He means to recompense the pains you take
By cutting off your heads: thus hath he sworn
And I with him, and many moe with me,
Upon the altar at Saint Edmundsbury;
Even on that altar where we swore to you
Dear amity and everlasting love.   20
        SAL. May this be possible? may this be true?
        MEL. Have I not hideous death within my view,
Retaining but a quantity of life,
Which bleeds away, even as a form of wax
Resolveth from his figure 'gainst the fire?
What in the world should make me now deceive,
Since I must lose the use of all deceit?
Why should I then be false, since it is true
That I must die here and live hence by truth?
I say again, if Lewis do win the day,   30
He is forsworn, if e'er those eyes of yours
Behold another day break in the east:

---

7 *revolts*] men in revolt, deserters.
10 *bought and sold*] tricked, befooled, betrayed.
11 *Unthread the rude eye*] Undo the evil, redress the wrong.
14 *loud*] boisterous, stormy.
15 *He*] i.e., The Dauphin.
17 *moe*] an old form of "more."
23 *quantity*] small quantity, modicum.
24 *a form of wax*] a model or effigy of wax. Witches were credited with the
    practice of modelling a waxen figure of one whom they destined for de-
    struction, and of causing the life to ebb as they melted the wax effigy be-
    fore a fire.
25 *Resolveth from*] Dissolveth, melteth.
29 *hence*] in heaven.

But even this night, whose black contagious breath
Already smokes about the burning crest
Of the old, feeble and day-wearied sun,
Even this ill night, your breathing shall expire,
Paying the fine of rated treachery
Even with a treacherous fine of all your lives,
If Lewis by your assistance win the day.
Commend me to one Hubert with your king: 40
The love of him, and this respect besides,
For that my grandsire was an Englishman,
Awakes my conscience to confess all this.
In lieu whereof, I pray you, bear me hence
From forth the noise and rumour of the field,
Where I may think the remnant of my thoughts
In peace, and part this body and my soul
With contemplation and devout desires.
   SAL. We do believe thee: and beshrew my soul
But I do love the favour and the form   50
Of this most fair occasion, by the which
We will untread the steps of damned flight,
And like a bated and retired flood,
Leaving our rankness and irregular course,
Stoop low within those bounds we have o'erlook'd,
And calmly run on in obedience
Even to our ocean, to our great King John.
My arm shall give thee help to bear thee hence;
For I do see the cruel pangs of death
Right in thine eye. Away, my friends! New flight;   60
And happy newness, that intends old right.
                                   [Exeunt, leading off Melun.

---

37 *rated treachery*] treachery which has been duly appraised or assessed, to which
    a fixed penalty or fine has been allotted.
41 *respect*] consideration.
44 *In lieu whereof*] In return for which.
45 *rumour*] commotion, roar.
50 *favour*] aspect.
53 *bated*] diminished, baffled.
54 *rankness*] exuberance, overflow.
61 *intends old right*] aims at establishing old right.

SCENE V. *The French Camp.*

Enter LEWIS *and his train*

LEW. The sun of heaven methought was loath to set,
But stay'd, and made the western welkin blush,
When English measure backward their own ground
In faint retire. O, bravely came we off,
When with a volley of our needless shot,
After such bloody toil, we bid good night;
And wound our tottering colours clearly up,
Last in the field, and almost lords of it!

Enter a Messenger

MESS. Where is my prince, the Dauphin?
LEW.   Here: what news?
MESS. The Count Melun is slain; the English lords   10
By his persuasion are again fall'n off,
And your supply, which you have wish'd so long,
Are cast away and sunk on Goodwin Sands.
    LEW. Ah, foul shrewd news! beshrew thy very heart!
I did not think to be so sad to-night
As this hath made me. Who was he that said
King John did fly an hour or two before
The stumbling night did part our weary powers?
    MESS. Whoever spoke it, it is true, my lord.
    LEW. Well; keep good quarter and good care to-night: 20
The day shall not be up so soon as I,
To try the fair adventure of to-morrow.   [*Exeunt.*

---

4 *came we off*] we escaped.
7 *And wound ... clearly up*] And completely furled our flags, which hung or
    waved limply (after the severe action of the day).
11 *fall'n off*] revolted.
14 *shrewd ... beshrew*] bitter or cursed ... curse.
18 *stumbling night*] night which causes stumbling.
20 *good quarter*] strict guard.

SCENE VI. *An Open Place in the Neighbourhood of Swinstead Abbey.*

Enter the BASTARD *and* HUBERT, *severally*

HUB. Who's there? speak, ho! speak quickly, or I shoot.

BAST. A friend. What art thou?

HUB.   Of the part of England.

BAST. Whither dost thou go?

HUB. What's that to thee? why may not I demand
Of thine affairs, as well as thou of mine?

BAST. Hubert, I think.

HUB.   Thou hast a perfect thought:
I will upon all hazards well believe
Thou art my friend, that know'st my tongue so well.   10
Who art thou?

BAST.   Who thou wilt: and if thou please,
Thou mayst befriend me so much as to think
I come one way of the Plantagenets.

HUB. Unkind remembrance! thou and eyeless night
Have done me shame: brave soldier, pardon me,
That any accent breaking from thy tongue
Should 'scape the true acquaintance of mine ear.

BAST. Come, come; sans compliment, what news abroad?

HUB. Why, here walk I in the black brow of night,
To find you out.

BAST.   Brief, then; and what's the news?

HUB. O, my sweet sir, news fitting to the night,
Black, fearful, comfortless and horrible.   20

BAST. Show me the very wound of this ill news:
I am no woman, I'll not swoon at it.

HUB. The king, I fear, is poison'd by a monk:
I left him almost speechless; and broke out
To acquaint you with this evil, that you might
The better arm you to the sudden time,
Than if you had at leisure known of this.

---

2 *Of the part*] On the side.

12 *eyeless*] blind, dark: Theobald's emendation of the Folio reading *endless*.

26 *to the sudden time*] to meet the emergency at once.

Bast. How did he take it? who did taste to him?

Hub. A monk, I tell you; a resolved villain,
Whose bowels suddenly burst out: the king   30
Yet speaks and peradventure may recover.

Bast. Who didst thou leave to tend his majesty?

Hub. Why, know you not? the lords are all come back,
And brought Prince Henry in their company;
At whose request the king hath pardon'd them,
And they are all about his majesty.

Bast. Withhold thine indignation, mighty heaven,
And tempt us not to bear above our power!
I'll tell thee, Hubert, half my power this night,
Passing these flats, are taken by the tide;   40
These Lincoln Washes have devoured them;
Myself, well mounted, hardly have escaped.
Away before: conduct me to the king;
I doubt he will be dead or ere I come.   [*Exeunt.*

Scene VII. *The Orchard at Swinstead Abbey.*

Enter Prince Henry, Salisbury, *and* Bigot

P. Hen. It is too late: the life of all his blood
Is touch'd corruptibly, and his pure brain,
Which some suppose the soul's frail dwelling-house,
Doth by the idle comments that it makes
Foretell the ending of mortality.

Enter Pembroke

Pem. His highness yet doth speak, and holds belief
That, being brought into the open air,
It would allay the burning quality

---

28 *taste*] test the purity of the food by tasting.
29 *resolved*] resolute, determined.
44 *doubt*] fear.
2 *corruptibly*] so as to cause corruption; malignantly (in the medical sense).

Of that fell poison which assaileth him.

P. HEN. Let him be brought into the orchard here.   10
Doth he still rage?   [*Exit Bigot.*

PEM.   He is more patient
Than when you left him; even now he sung.

P. HEN. O vanity of sickness! fierce extremes
In their continuance will not feel themselves.
Death, having prey'd upon the outward parts,
Leaves them invisible, and his siege is now
Against the mind, the which he pricks and wounds
With many legions of strange fantasies,
Which, in their throng and press to that last hold,
Confound themselves. 'T is strange that death should sing.   20
I am the cygnet to this pale faint swan,
Who chants a doleful hymn to his own death,
And from the organ-pipe of frailty sings
His soul and body to their lasting rest.

SAL. Be of good comfort, prince; for you are born
To set a form upon that indigest
Which he hath left so shapeless and so rude.

Enter Attendants, *and* BIGOT, *carrying* KING JOHN *in a chair*

K. JOHN. Ay, marry, now my soul hath elbow-room;
It would not out at windows nor at doors.
There is so hot a summer in my bosom,   30
That all my bowels crumble up to dust:
I am a scribbled form, drawn with a pen
Upon a parchment, and against this fire
Do I shrink up.

P. HEN.   How fares your majesty?

K. JOHN. Poison'd,—ill fare—dead, forsook, cast off:
And none of you will bid the winter come

13–14 *fierce extremes … feel themselves*] the worst pangs of illness, when they
     persist, cease to give the sensation of bodily suffering; they tend to render
     the mere flesh unconscious, insensible.
16 *Leaves them invisible*] Death, having worked its evil will on the bodily or-
     gans, passes from them to besiege or attack the mind.
19 *in their throng … hold*] in their tumult and hurry to reach the last tenable part
     of the dying man.
26 *indigest*] crude chaotic mass.

To thrust his icy fingers in my maw,
Nor let my kingdom's rivers take their course
Through my burn'd bosom, nor entreat the north
To make his bleak winds kiss my parched lips   40
And comfort me with cold. I do not ask you much,
I beg cold comfort; and you are so strait
And so ingrateful, you deny me that.

    P. HEN. O that there were some virtue in my tears,
That might relieve you!

    K. JOHN.   The salt in them is hot.
Within me is a hell; and there the poison
Is as a fiend confined to tyrannize
On unreprieveable condemned blood.

Enter the BASTARD

    BAST. O, I am scalded with my violent motion,
And spleen of speed to see your majesty!   50

    K. JOHN. O cousin, thou art come to set mine eye:
The tackle of my heart is crack'd and burn'd,
And all the shrouds wherewith my life should sail
Are turned to one thread, one little hair:
My heart hath one poor string to stay it by,
Which holds but till thy news be uttered;
And then all this thou seest is but a clod
And module of confounded royalty.

    BAST. The Dauphin is preparing hitherward,
Where heaven He knows how we shall answer him;   60
For in a night the best part of my power,
As I upon advantage did remove,
Were in the Washes all unwarily
Devoured by the unexpected flood.   [*The king dies.*

    SAL. You breathe these dead news in as dead an ear.
My liege! my lord! but now a king, now thus.

    P. HEN. Even so must I run on, and even so stop.
What surety of the world, what hope, what stay,
When this was now a king, and now is clay?

---

42 *strait*] niggardly.
58 *module of confounded royalty*] mould of ruined royalty.
60 *answer him*] meet his attack.
62 *upon advantage did remove*] moved the troops on the occurrence of (what seemed to be) a favourable opportunity.

BAST. Art thou gone so? I do but stay behind   70
To do the office for thee of revenge,
And then my soul shall wait on thee to heaven,
As it on earth hath been thy servant still.
Now, now, you stars that move in your right spheres,
Where be your powers? show now your mended faiths,
And instantly return with me again,
To push destruction and perpetual shame
Out of the weak door of our fainting land.
Straight let us seek, or straight we shall be sought;
The Dauphin rages at our very heels.   80
   SAL. It seems you know not, then, so much as we:
The Cardinal Pandulph is within at rest,
Who half an hour since came from the Dauphin,
And brings from him such offers of our peace
As we with honour and respect may take,
With purpose presently to leave this war.
   BAST. He will the rather do it when he sees
Ourselves well sinewed to our defence.
   SAL. Nay, it is in a manner done already;
For many carriages he hath dispatch'd   90
To the sea-side, and put his cause and quarrel
To the disposing of the cardinal:
With whom yourself, myself and other lords,
If you think meet, this afternoon will post
To consummate this business happily.
   BAST. Let it be so: and you, my noble prince,
With other princes that may best be spared,
Shall wait upon your father's funeral.
   P. HEN. At Worcester must his body be interr'd;
For so he will'd it.
   BAST.   Thither shall it then: 100
And happily may your sweet self put on
The lineal state and glory of the land!
To whom, with all submission, on my knee
I do bequeath my faithful services

---

82 *The Cardinal Pandulph ... at rest*] As a matter of history, Pandulph had lately
    been succeeded as legate by Gualo, who finally negotiated peace.
97 *princes*] possibly an accidental error for *nobles*. The word seems wrongly
    repeated from the line before.
104 *bequeath*] transfer.

And true subjection everlastingly.

    SAL. And the like tender of our love we make,
To rest without a spot for evermore.

    P. HEN. I have a kind soul that would give you thanks
And knows not how to do it but with tears.

    BAST. O, let us pay the time but needful woe,   110
Since it hath been beforehand with our griefs.
This England never did, nor never shall,
Lie at the proud foot of a conqueror,
But when it first did help to wound itself.
Now these her princes are come home again,
Come the three corners of the world in arms,
And we shall shock them. Nought shall make us rue,
If England to itself do rest but true.   *[Exeunt.*

110–111 *O, let us pay...griefs*] O, let us pay the events no more than the
    essential due of mourning, since time has prefaced the catastrophe with
    afflictions enough.
116 *three corners of the world*] The reference is apparently to the three known
    continents—Europe, Africa, and Asia.